Progressive Civility

Westphalia Press Civility Series

westphaliapress.org

Volume 1
Revolutionary Civility
Rules of Decent Behavior in Company and Conversation

Volume 2
Expansive Civility
The American Chesterfield

Volume 3
Manifest Civility
The Young Man's Own Book

Volume 4
Industrial Civility
The Primer of Politeness

Volume 5
Progressive Civility
Wehman's Etiquette and Politeness

Volume 6
Civility and the Great War
The Stakes of Diplomacy

Volume 7
Postwar Civility
On Kindness

Progressive Civility

Wehman's Etiquette and Politeness

by Henry J. Wehman

Volume 5 in the Westphalia Press Civility Series

WESTPHALIA PRESS
An imprint of Policy Studies Organization

Westphalia Press
An imprint of Policy Studies Organization
1527 New Hampshire Ave., NW
Washington, D.C. 20036
dgutierrezs@ipsonet.org

ISBN-13: 978-1935907619
ISBN-10: 1935907611

Cover design by Taillefer Long at Illuminated Stories:
www.illuminatedstories.com

Updated material and comments on this edition
can be found at the Westphalia Press website:
www.westphaliapress.org

In Search of Civility

An archaic meaning of civility was 'study of the humanities,' and as a word it appears in the sixteenth century. The years have not blunted its importance; it is one of the guiding principles of *Wikipedia*, which informs readers that, "The civility policy is a standard of conduct that sets out how *Wikipedia* editors should interact. Stated simply, editors should always treat each other with consideration and respect. In order to keep the focus on improving the encyclopedia and to help maintain a pleasant editing environment, editors should behave politely, calmly and reasonably, even during heated debates."

Other voices also have been raised about the need to consider civility as a priority in an increasingly abrasive modern society. The Institute for Civility in Government in Houston, ably led by Cassandra Dahnke and Tomas Spath, has for many years hosted Washington seminars and blogs on the subject. Profesor J.M. Forni at Johns Hopkins has made a life's work out of studying the ramifications of civility. In the Hopkins alumni magazine he sums the current situation up when he writes:

E

We do have our manners. What we have lost are the manners of past generations. That we have manners, however, does not mean we ought to be perfectly happy with the manners we have. In fact, many Americans think that civility and manners are in decline, that this decline has increased in the past several years, and that there is a causal connection between incivility and violence. Does reality match the perception of a decline? Yes and no. There is little doubt that we are losing established forms of deference and respect. On the other hand, new forms of respect take the place of those becoming obsolete. A pregnant woman may not easily find a youngster willing to give her his seat on a bus. But the number of men willing to treat the same woman as an intellectual peer on the job is higher today than it was yesterday.

This does not mean that we should ignore the coarsening of social interaction that we have been witnessing in recent years. Our manners inevitably suffer when:

1. We are poorly trained in self-restraint.

2. We are used to seeing others as means to the satisfaction of our desires rather than ends in themselves.

3. We are overly concerned about financial gain and professional achievement.

4. We are constantly besieged by stress and fatigue.

5. We are surrounded by strangers who will remain strangers.

When some or all of these factors are at work, it becomes difficult to be considerate — and consideration is the ethical requirement of manners that are really good.

Clearly we need more people to take an interest in the topic rather than less. The Westphalia Press Civility Series demonstrates that the topic has many aspects, including etiquette and diplomacy. My friend Ambassador Mark Hambley suggests that there even might be some connection between the decline of cursive writing and the decline of civility. Unfortunately the current lack of civility in Washington is as noticeable or more noticeable than the state of the nation's handwriting. While politics has always been a competitive sport, common consensus is that the political life in the capital recently has become far more contentious than in recent memory.

F

The Westphalia Press Civility Series presents manners, etiquette, diplomacy, decent behavior, and politeness as fruit in the same orchard. The books are intended to be an accessible resource for studying facets of a subject that we think contributes to the current policy anxiety that has paralyzed decision making.

The subject has a universal aspect. Although we relish including George Washington as author of one of the titles in the collection, he actually found many of the maxims in his *Rules of Civility* in the literature of French Jesuits of the 1590s that was rendered in English by Francis Hawkins in London in 1640. By all account he was a man of manners no matter what the circumstances, and so we respectfully dedicate this series to his memory, in hopes that present day leaders will reflect on his example.

Paul Rich
President, Policy Studies Organization
Garfield House, Washington, D.C.

H

WEHMAN'S

NEW

BOOK

ON

ETIQUETTE

AND POLITENESS

NEW YORK.
HENRY J. WEHMAN, PUBLISHER,
108 PARK ROW.

WEHMAN'S

NEW BOOK ON

Etiquette and Politeness.

A PERFECT GUIDE

TO

POLITE SOCIETY,

ITS

CUSTOMS AND USAGES.

PLAIN. CONCISE. RELIABLE.

NEW YORK:
HENRY J. WEHMAN, PUBLISHER,
PARK ROW.

1890.

PREFATORY.

Of books there are many, and among them a large number devoted to Etiquette and the usages of society, in which are presented rules for the general government thereof and proper deportment at all times and on each and every occasion. A glance through their pages prove them to be, for the most part, perfunctory, while much therein contained has become obsolete through the ever-varying changes wrought by advancement in intellectuality and the arts. The objective in this book has been the winnowing of the chaff from the wheat, and to present a code of rules in a plain and concise manner. As an epitome of all that is valuable, it is sent forth with the assurance that it will be of invaluable interest to every one who consults its pages; and that the adoption of the lessons it inculcates will prove a ready passport to genteel society, and secure perfect freedom from constraint in every walk of life.

CONTENTS.

WEHMAN'S

NEW BOOK ON

ETIQUETTE AND POLITENESS.

General Observations.

Etiquette and Politeness are synonyms of true principles established to regulate our conduct towards others, so as not to give offense or cause a disagreeable feeling—never to show our temper or make a remark that we think will create an unpleasant sensation to the listeners, and on all occasions to religiously refrain from gratuitous intrusions of whatever nature. You should always show a genuine kindness of heart, cultivate a correct taste, and possess such self-control as never to be rude or discourteous to any one, however far he may transgress conventional usages. Lacking these qualities, the most perfect knowledge of the rules of etiquette, and the strict observance of them, will not suffice to make you a perfect gentleman or lady.

To appear as a man of merit you must be necessarily a gentleman. Not a man of birth, as is sometimes meant by gentle, but a man of culture and refinement—such culture and refinement as are within the reach of every man who chooses to make the necessary effort to acquire them. It is the highest praise that can be bestowed upon a man, "He is a thorough gentleman." When you have thus spoken of a man you have tersely accorded him everything that is becoming a man. On the other hand the essence of all that is unmanly and ungenerous is summed up in the exclamation, "He is no gentleman." That expression comprehends cowards, blackguards, braggarts, and all those who have a mean spirit, though polished with the most distinguished lustre of manner, and shining with the most splendid ornaments.

Education is a distinguishing mark of a gentleman. It is not absolutely necessary that it should be classical, or embrace a knowledge of ancient or foreign tongues; but so far as it goes it should be sound. A well informed man is welcome in most circles; but not a man who bores with his information. There are certain subjects on which every one is supposed to be capable of speaking. A slight acquaintance with works of art and with the music and literature of the day is indispensable in society.

A gentleman has a perfect control over his temper. It is a mark of good breeding to avoid argument on points likely to lead to the expres-

5

sion of strong feelings, especially on religious and political topics, but should these be introduced, a gentleman will not discuss them with warmth.

Morals lay the foundation of manners. A well ordered mind, a well regulated heart, produce the best conduct. The rules which a philosopher or moralist lays down for his own guidance, properly developed, lead to the most courteous acts. Franklin laid down the following rules to regulate his conduct through life:

Temperance.—Eat not to dullness; drink not to elevation.

Silence.—Speak not but what may benefit others or yourself; avoid trifling conversation.

Order.—Let all your things have their places; let each part of your business have its time.

Resolution.—Resolve to perform what you ought; perform without fail what you resolve.

Frugality.—Make no expense but to do good to others, or to yourself; *i. e.,* waste nothing.

Industry.—Lose no time; be always employed in something useful; cut off all unnecessary actions.

Sincerity.—Use no hurtful deceit; think innocently and justly; and if you speak, speak accordingly.

Justice.—Wrong none by doing injuries, or omitting the benefits that are your duty.

Moderation.—Avoid extremes; forbear resenting injuries, so much as you think they deserve.

Cleanliness.—Tolerate no uncleanliness in body, clothes, or habitation.

Tranquillity.—Be not disturbed at trifles, or at accidents common or unavoidable, and "be temperate in all things."

Let these rules be applied to the elegant intercourse of life, and they are precisely what is required. Those who would set good morals and good manners at variance, wrong both.

Perfect ease and tranquillity of manner are the signs of good breeding. Persons who move in the higher circles of life, and who have a proper regard for appearances, never allow themselves to appear vexed or disturbed. They study to appear composed, whatever may occur to annoy them, and are not thrown into a state of excitement by every petty trifle.

If you see a man behave in an uncivil manner to his father or mother, his brother or sister, wife or children, or fail to exercise, when dining *en famille,* the common courtesies of life at his own table, you may at once set him down as a boor, for good manners are articles for everyday wear.

Do not fall into the absurd error of supposing you may do as you please at home. Have a proper regard for the feelings and comfort not only of your own family, but of your servants. The true gentleman and the true gentlewoman are never arrogant or overbearing to domestics or *employees*. Their commands are requests, and all services, no matter how humble, are received with thanks, as if they were favors. There is no surer sign of vulgarity than an assumption of the tone of authority, a haughty or supercilious demeanor towards inferiors in station.

Another thing to avoid is an ostentatious display of magnificence. Over-dressed people are always vulgar. A house that looks as if it had been furnished as an upholsterer's show room only serves to make the owner ridiculous. In dress and in furniture good manners dictate a strict regard to propriety; everything good, everything in keeping, everything indicating an acquaintance with the prevailing fashion, but nothing to dazzle the eyes and excite astonishment in the simple.

Well-bred people are at home everywhere, and possess in a high degree the faculty of making other people feel at home. Very different is it with that "stuck up" community whose only idea of etiquette seems to begin and end with an assertion of their own importance. They are at home nowhere, and no one is at home with them; they seem to be forever rattling their money, and inviting you to look at their cheque-book; they promenade their rooms with the manners of a cicerone; and they call your special attention to the viands and wines spread for your entertainment. The pronoun "my" is forever on their lips, and their pæan of self-praise never sounds so meanly as when it is heard in the key of self-appreciation. A man of uncultivated manners utters all his mind, storms and fumes at every trifling occurrence, falls out with everybody, is noisy and imperious, manifesting his presence by loud and boisterous talking. With a noisy step he enters the room, sits down or stands up in a noisy manner; when he moves a chair, he causes it to knock against the floor; when he ascends the stairs, he tramps like a cart-horse. Feeling abashed, although he has done nothing to be ashamed of, he does not know how to comport himself so as to appear easy or elude observation. In this dilemma he shifts, shuffles, and tries various ways of sitting or standing. His most common resource is meddling with his hair, or touching some part of his face. This gives employment to his hands, and has, as he thinks, a look of being at ease, while in reality it is quite the reverse. In all good society it is considered exceedingly bad manners to touch either the hair or any part of the head or countenance with the hands. Picking the nails, scratching or rubbing any part of the body or limbs, putting your fingers in your ears, and similar indecencies of behavior are equally inconsistent with good manners. They are actions which are exceedingly offensive to spectators, and are therefore carefully shunned by all persons possessing the slightest sense of propriety.

Etiquette is, in point of fact, the *summum bonum*, the written and unwritten law, which regulates the society of civilized people, distinguishing them from the communities of barbarous tribes, whose lives are hard and their manners still harder. It is to a well disciplined and refined mind the fundamental principle of action in all intercourse with society.

Etiquette, like every other human institution, is of course liable to abuse; it may be transformed from a convenient and wholesome means of producing universal comfort into an inconvenient and burdensome restraint upon freedom and ease. It may become the first consideration instead of more properly the second, and then it becomes an intolerable nuisance. The mere form, overriding and hiding the spirit which should control and hide it; an entirely artificial state of things, taking the place of the natural, must inevitably produce discomfort and extravagance of behavior. Nature is thus made the slave of Art, instead of Art taking its proper place as the handmaid of Nature. Etiquette, to be perfect, therefore, must be like a perfectly fitting garment, which, beautifying and adorning the person, must yet never cramp or restrain perfect freedom of movement. Any visible restraint will mar its grace, as a wrinkle will mar the pure outline of the garment.

If all this be true of mankind, how still more true is it of womankind! Granted that truthfulness, gracefulness, unselfishness, are essential to the breeding of a true gentleman, how infinitely essential must they be to the breeding of a true lady! That her tact should be even readier, her sympathies even tenderer, her instinct even finer than those of the man, seems only fit and natural. In her politeness and all the minor observances of etiquette are absolutely indispensable. She must be even more upon her guard than a man in all those niceties of speech, look and manner which are the especial and indispensable credentials of good breeding. Every little drawing room ceremonial, all the laws of society, the whole etiquette of hospitality must be familiar to her. And even in these points, artificial though they be, her best guide after all is that kindness of heart which gives honor where honor is due and which is ever anxious to spare the feelings and prejudices of others.

Every mistress of a house is a minor sovereign, upon whose bounty the comfort and happiness and refinement of her little court depends. She must take especial care that her servants are capable, well trained and reliable, and that her domestic arrangements are carried on as noiselessly and easily as if by machinery. In a well ordered house the machinery is always in order, and always works out of sight. No well-bred woman talks of her servants, of her dinner arrangements, or the affairs of her nursery. One feels these matters to be under her *surveillance*, and that fact alone is a guarantee of their good management. The amusements and comforts of her guests are provided for without discussion or comment; and whatever goes wrong is studiously withheld from the conversation of the drawing-room. And let no lady, however young, however beautiful, however gifted, for one moment imagine that the management of her house can be neglected with impunity. If she is rich enough to provide an efficient housekeeper, well and good; but, even so, the final responsibility must still rest upon her, and her alone. No tastes, no pleasures must stand in the way of this important duty; and even if that duty should at first seem irksome, the fulfillment of it is sure to bring its own reward.

The very atmosphere of the house proclaims the mistress. The servants wear a cheerful air, and meet you with candid and friendly faces; the rooms are tastefully furnished; and irreproachable cleanliness and neatness reign around. The unexpected guest finds an orderly table and an unembarrassed welcome. In such a house, scandal finds no favor, and conversation never degenerates into gossip. In such a home, peace and plenty and good will are permanent household gods.

And in this connection I will cite some recent conversations between some eminent ladies in our land, as to what constitutes the "Perfect Lady." In reply to the question a very prominent lady replied:

"Girls should imbibe good manners without much teaching, but there is one quality that mothers should impress on their daughters, and that is that they should always consider other people's pleasure before their own. I am sure that this is the one thing lacking in the well-bred girl, and I have been pained beyond measure by seeing girls when they were introduced to any person who, for some reason, they did not consider their equal, bow coldly without one kindly word of greeting, and turn the head to continue their interrupted conversation with some friend. That has happened at my receptions, and it occurred once or twice when I myself have made the introduction."

"Disrespect to any caller at my house is disrespect to me, and I have decided never to recognize girls whom I have seen guilty of this breach of kindliness if not of etiquette. I am fond of young girls and I like to see them winning and cordial in their manner to the most humble person who comes into their presence. They can find ample time to enjoy their friends' society in their own drawing-rooms, but when they are in any home to assist the hostess they should make courtesy to their guests the first consideration."

"I always think when I see any one disdainful of those whom they meet of the story of Washington when he met his colored man-servant and raised his hat in response to the man's salutation. Some one said to him:

"Is it possible, Gen. Washington, that you raise your hat to your slave?'

"'Yes, always, for I will not have a slave outdo me in politeness.'"

"To me," continued the lady, "that is the most essential lesson a girl can learn, and if she remembers that story well, older people will never have to blush for her, and," with a little laugh, "I will not have to debar her from my house."

Another lady agreed with the former, that "the unkindliest custom in Washington, the capital of the nation, is that of not making any introductions." In talking of it she related a little incident of how, when she first went to the capital as a member's wife, she took a friend with her to call upon a lady high up in the official scale and who had just returned from abroad. They entered the room, were received willingly by the hostess, who soon had to give her whole attention to some new arrivals. The ladies who were receiving with her looked at them coldly, chatted among themselves, and they drifted through the rooms, fairly ostracized because they chanced not to know any one.

"We soon took our departure, and the lady who was with me said: 'If this is the hospitality for which Washington is so famous I will have none of it,' and I never again, when she returned for a visit, could persuade her to go with me to that house. I always introduce people who enter my drawing room, and who I see are strangers, if for no other reason than because I do not want them to feel as miserable as I did at my first call at that house."

And here is how another defines a "perfect lady":

"A woman may be cultivated, accomplished, stylish and thoroughly au fait in all the forms and customs of polite society and still be lacking in the essential qualities that make a lady. On the other hand, a true lady may be neither stylish nor accustomed to society, but she will grace any occasion she may honor by her presence. The true lady possesses the refinement of the heart and soul that reveals itself in every action. In training a daughter a mother should endeavor to instill kindness of heart and thoughtfulness of others and to be thoroughly unselfish."

A lady who is the wife of a former President of the land is thus portrayed as the ideal:

"Mrs. ——'s simplicity of manner was what made her the perfect lady," said she, "although I think even that would not have made her so dearly loved if she had not had with it a gentle dignity which kept her from being confused in the most trying situations. A woman who is easily flustered, no matter what her other charms, can never appear the well-bred woman. I saw her in society, where she was both guest and hostess, I saw her in the privacy of her life, and I think I never, no matter how familiar I became with her qualities, missed expressing to myself, or whoever was with me, my admiration for her uniform affability and gentleness."

And yet another lady being asked "Who is a perfect lady"? said:

"Who is a Christian? you might as well ask, for the two are about the same. It is easier to say, Who is not a well-bred woman, and first of all I would say that it is not the woman who speaks shrilly or crossly to her servants or those under her. In many a parlor I have heard a mistress order her servants about in a way that has made me conclude that whatever other attribute of a lady she may have, she was woefully lacking in one. The best of a woman is not seen in a drawing-room, and polish injures rather than improves ladylike characteristics. I have seen the kindliest woman in the world polished until she became a very flint. The woman who is constantly willing to forget herself and look out for the happiness of other people is the one who will most quickly receive the title of 'Lady'."

The most perfect law of politeness, the safest and surest guide in all that pertains to the true definition of a gentleman or lady is, after all, the Christian rule—"Do unto others as you would others should do unto you." No one with this for a guide can ever fail in true, genuine politeness, and that politeness will soon lead him to learn and remember all the prevailing rules of established etiquette.

Introductions.

To introduce persons who are mutually unknown is to undertake a serious responsibility, and to certify to each the respectability of the other. Never undertake this responsibility without, in the first place, asking yourself whether the persons are likely to be agreeable to each other; nor, in the second place, without ascertaining whether it will be acceptible to both parties to become acquainted.

Always introduce the gentleman to the lady—never the lady to the gentleman. The chivalry of etiquette assumes that the lady is invariably the superior in right of her sex, and that the gentleman is honored by the introduction.

Never present a gentleman to a lady without first asking her permission to do so.

When you are introduced to a lady, never offer your hand. When introduced, persons limit their recognition of each other to a bow.

Persons who have met at the house of a mutual friend without being introduced, should not bow if they afterwards meet elsewhere; a bow implies acquaintance, and persons who have not been introduced are not acquainted.

If you are walking with one friend, and presently meet with, or are joined by, a second, do not commit the too frequent error of introducing them to each other. You have even less right to do so then if they encountered each other at your house during a morning call.

There are some exceptions to the etiquette of introductions. At a ball or evening party, where there is dancing, the mistress of the house may introduce any gentleman to any lady without first asking the lady's permission. But she should first ascertain whether the lady is willing to dance; and this out of consideration for the gentleman, who may otherwise be refused. No man likes to be refused the hand of a lady, though it be only for a quadrille.

A brother may present his sister, or a father his son, without any kind of preliminary; but only when there is no inferiority on the part of his own family to that of the acquaintance.

Friends may introduce friends at the house of a mutual acquaintance, but, as a rule, it is better to be introduced by the mistress of the house. Such an introduction carries more authority with it.

Introductions at evening parties are now almost wholly dispensed with. Persons who meet at a friend's house are ostensibly upon an equality, and pay a bad compliment to the host by appearing suspicious and formal. Some oldfashioned country hosts yet persevere in introducing each newcomer to all the assembled guests. It is a custom that cannot be too soon abolished, and one that places the last unfortunate visitor in a singularly awkward position. All that he can do is to make a semi-circular bow, and bear the general gaze with as much composure as possible.

If, when you enter a drawing room, your name has been wrongly announced, or has passed unheard in the buzz of conversation, make your way at once to the mistress of the house, if you are a stranger, and introduce yourself by name. This should be done with the greatest simplicity, and your professional or titular rank made as little of as possible.

An introduction given at a ball for the mere purpose of conducting a lady through a dance does not give the gentleman any right to bow to her on a future occasion. If he commits this error, he must remember that she is not bound to see or return his salutation.

Should you find an agreeable person in private society, who seems desirous of making your acquaintance, there cannot be any objection to your meeting his advances half way, although the ceremony of an introduction may not have taken place.

If you meet a male acquaintance in the street, accompanied by a lady, either raise or take off your hat to him, instead of nodding. This last familiar mode of recognition looks disrespectful towards her.

An adherence to etiquette is a mark of respect; if a man be worth knowing, he is surely worth the trouble to approach properly. It will likewise relieve you from the awkwardness of being acquainted with people of whom you might at times be ashamed, or be obliged under many circumstances to "cut."

The act of "cutting" can only be justified by some strong instance of bad conduct in the person to be cut. A cold bow, which discourages familiarity without offering insult, is the best mode to adopt towards those with whom an acquaintance is not deemed desirable. An increased observance of ceremony is, however, the most delicate way of withdrawing from an acquaintance; and the person so treated must be obtuse, indeed, who does not take the hint. And when you observe that any of your own acquaintances appear distant and more than usually ceremonious towards you, you may suspect that they desire to withdraw their intimacy, if not their friendship.

When you are introduced to a person, be careful not to appear as though you had never heard of him before. If he happens to be a person of any distinction, such a mistake would be unpardonable, and no person is complimented by being reminded of the fact that his name is unknown.

If, when walking with one friend, you should meet another, it is not necessary to introduce them; indeed, you should not do so without special reason for it. Never, even after an introduction, start a long conversation, unless all continue the walk in the same direction.

Should you, when walking with a friend, meet a lady who desires to speak to you, your friend must stop with you, yet an introduction under such circumstances does not exact any future recognition.

It is best to avoid introductions in a public conveyance, as few people like to have their names called out in such places. If such introductions are made, however, it should be done as quietly as possible.

To introduce to a friend a person who is in any way objectionable, is an insult which fully justifies a withdrawal of friendship.

In visiting foreign courts, introductions are more a matter of ceremony than in this country. If you wish to obtain an introduction to the Emperor of Austria, you must address your request to the Grand Chamberlain, which may be done personally or by letter.

Your statement that you are an American citizen, and a reference to the American Consul will procure you an interview. Punctuality to the hour appointed for the interview is essential, and ladies present themselves in full dress; gentlemen in a dress suit of black, white vest, gloves and neck-tie.

The ceremony of presentation will be explained before you are presented.

In the English court, the ladies must be presented by a lady; gentlemen by a gentleman. Strangers must have credentials from the Consul before they can be introduced.

Letters of Introduction.

Do not lightly give or promise letters of introduction. Always remember that when you give a letter of introduction you lay yourself under an obligation to the friend to whom it is addressed. If your friend lives in a great city, you in a measure compel that friend to undergo the penalty of escorting the stranger to some of those places of public entertainment in which the city abounds. If your friend be a married lady, and the mistress of a house, you put her to the expense of inviting the stranger to her table. We cannot be too cautious how we tax the time and purse of a friend, or weigh too seriously the question of mutual advantage in the introduction. Always ask yourself whether the person introduced will be an acceptable acquaintance to the one to whom you present them; and whether the pleasure of knowing them will compensate for the time or money which it costs to entertain them. If the stranger is in any unsuitable in habits or temperament, you inflict an annoyance on your friend instead of a pleasure. In questions of introduction never oblige one friend to the discomfort of another.

Those to whom letters of introduction have been given should send them to the person to whom they are addressed, and enclose a card. Avoid delivering a letter of introduction in person. It places you in the most undignified position imaginable, and compels you to wait while it is being read, like a servant who has been told to wait for an answer. If the receiver of the letter be a really well-bred person, they will call upon you or leave their card the next day, and you should return their attention within the week.

If, on the other hand, a stranger sends you a letter of introduction and their card, you are bound by the laws of politeness and hospitality, not only to call upon them the next day, but to follow up that attention with others. If you are in a position to do so, the most correct thing is to invite them to dine with you. Should this not be within your power, you can probably escort them to some of the exhibitions, private collections, club houses, theatres, or reading rooms. In short, etiquette demands that you shall exert yourself to show kindness to the stranger, if only out of compliment to the friend.

A letter of introduction should be given unsealed, not alone because your friend may wish to know what you have said, but also as a guarantee of your own good faith. As you should never give such a letter unless you can speak highly of the bearer, this rule of etiquette is easy to observe. By requesting your friend to fasten the envelope before forwarding the letter to its destination, you tacitly give permission to inspect its contents.

Business letters of introduction should mention the errand and business of the party introduced.

Letters of introduction soliciting favors should be but seldom given, and never unless the claims upon both parties interested are very strong.

Visiting.

MORNING CALLS.

A morning visit should be paid between the hours of 3 and 5 P. M. By observing this rule you avoid intruding before the luncheon is removed, and leave in sufficient time for the lady of the house to have an hour or two of leisure for her drive and dinner toilette. Never pay a visit before noon; and be careful always to avoid the luncheon hours of your friends. Some ladies dine with their children at one or half-past one o'clock, and are consequently unprepared for the early reception of visitors. When you have once ascertained this to be the case, be careful never to intrude again at the same hour.

A good memory for these trifles is one of the hall-marks of good-breeding.

A first visit should be returned the next day; at latest within three days. A visit of ceremony—and, indeed, a visit of friendship—should always be brief. If even the conversation becomes animated, beware of letting your call exceed half an hour in length. It is better to let your friends regret rather than desire your withdrawal.

When returning visits of ceremony, you may, without impoliteness, leave your card at the door, without going in. Do not, however, fail to inquire if the family be well. Should there be daughters or sisters residing with the lady upon whom you call, leave a card for each. If there are visitors staying in the house, it is better to distinguish the cards intended for them by writing their names above your own. A married lady, calling upon a married lady, leaves her husband's card for the husband of her friend.

Unless when returning thanks for "kind inquiries," and announcing your arrival in, or departure from, town, it is not considered respectful to send round cards by a servant.

Visits of condolence are paid within the week after the event which occasions them. Personal visits of this kind are made only by relations and very intimate friends, who should be careful to make the conversation as little painful as possible.

In paying visits of congratulation, you should always go in, and be hearty in your congratulations. Wedding-cards are generally sent round to such people as one wishes to keep up acquaintance with, and these will call first on the newly-married pair. A visit is also due to the parents who have invited you to the wedding-breakfast.

A call should invariably be made within a week upon friends or acquaintances at whose house you have dined, or from whom you have received an invitation to dine.

A well-bred person will endeavor to receive visitors at any time. If you are occupied and cannot afford to be interrupted, it is better to instruct your servant to say that you are never "at home," except upon certain days and at certain hours. If a servant once admits a visitor within the hall, receive him at any inconvenience : but take care that the circumstance does not occur again. A lady should never keep a visitor waiting. Some ladies only receive visitors on a stated afternoon in each week; but this is a somewhat pretentious custom, only to be justified by the exigencies of a very lofty position. Umbrellas and overcoats should always be left in the hall.

When a gentleman makes a morning call, he should never leave his hat or riding-whip in the hall, but should take both into the room. To do otherwise would be to make himself too much at home. The hat should never be laid on a table, pianoforte, or any article of furniture, but must be held properly in the hand. If you are compelled to lay it aside, put it on the floor.

Never take favorite dogs into a drawing-room when you make a morning call. Their feet may be dusty, or they may bark at strangers, or, being of too friendly a disposition, may take the liberty of lying on a lady's gown, or jumping upon a velvet sofa or an easy chair. Besides, your friend may have a favorite cat already established before the fire, and in that case a battle may ensue. Many persons, too, have a constitutional antipathy to dogs, and others never allow their own to be seen in the reception-rooms. For all or any of these reasons, a visitor has no right to inflict upon his friend the society of his dog as well as of himself.

Neither is it well for a mother to take young children with her when she pays morning visits; their presence, unless they are unusually well-trained, can only be productive of anxiety to yourself and your hostess. She, while striving to amuse them, or to appear interested in them, is secretly anxious for the fate of her album, or the ornaments upon her *étagère;* while the mother is trembling lest her children should say or do something objectionable.

If you do not keep a closed carriage, you should never pay visits of ceremony in wet weather. To enter a drawing-room with mud-bespattered boots and damp clothes is a *faux pas* that no lady or gentleman will commit.

It has of late become customary to offer tea to those visitors who make their calls between the hours of four and five o'clock. Tea should be sent round, already poured out, with sugar basin and cream ewer, on a small waiter. Biscuits or bread-and-butter may accompany it.

On entering a crowded drawing-room, go at once to pay your respects to the lady of the house, and take the seat she indicates to you. A gentleman should take any vacant chair he may find, without troubling his hostess to think for him.

A gentleman ought to rise upon the entrance of ladies. A lady does not rise. It is not permissible to leave one's chair in order to get nearer the fire. As a general rule, an introduction is only followed by a bow, unless the persons to whom your hostess introduces you are her relations or very old friends, and for some special reason she desires that you should make their acquaintance. In this case you give your hand. A man has no right to take a lady's hand till it is offered. Two ladies shake hands gently and softly. A lady gives her hand to a gentleman, but does not shake his hand in return. Young ladies only bow to unmarried men. It is the privilege of a superior to offer or withhold his hand; an inferior should never be the first to extend the hand. Foreigners rarely shake hands, and then only with intimate friends.

If other visitors are announced and you have already remained as long as courtesy requires, wait till they are seated; then take leave of your hostess; bow politely to the newly-arrived guests; and retire. You will, perhaps, be urged to remain; but having once arisen, it is best to go. There is always a certain air of *gaucherie* in resuming your seat, and repeating the ceremony of leave-taking. If you have occasion to look at your watch during a call, ask permission to do so, and apologize for it on the plea of other appointments.

A gentleman should rise when any lady takes her leave, and, if in his own house, should escort her to her carriage.

In receiving morning visits, it is not necessary that a lady should lay aside the employment in which she may be engaged, particularly if it consist of light or ornamental needle-work. Politeness, however, requires that music, drawing, or any absorbing occupation, be at once abandoned. A well-bred lady pays equal attention to all her visitors, and endeavors to make conversation as general as possible. It is allowable to pay extra attention to any person of distinguished rank, extreme age, or world-wide reputation. To do homage to the rich, simply because they are rich, is a piece of snobbism which even the most amiable find it difficult to forgive.

A lady need not advance to receive visitors when announced, unless they are persons to whom she is desirous of testifying particular respect. It is sufficient if she rises, moves forward a single step to shake hands with them, and remains standing till they are seated.

When her visitors rise to take leave, she should rise also, and remain standing till they have quite left the room. It is not necessary to accompany them to the drawing-room door, but the bell should be rung in good time, that the servant may be ready in the hall to let them out.

A lady can never call upon a gentleman unless professionally or officially. To do so would be, not only a breach of good manners, but of strict propriety.

A lady should dress well, though not too richly, when she pays or receives morning visits. If she has a carriage at command, she may dress more elegantly than if she were on foot. A gentleman should always be well dressed. No one in the present day can afford to dress badly.

Always avoid the foolish practice of deprecating your own rooms, furniture, or viands, and expressing regrets that you have nothing better to offer. Neither should you go to the other extreme of extolling any particular thing or article of food. The best way is to say nothing about these matters. Neither is it proper to urge guests to eat, or to load their plates against their inclinations.

Endeavor to retain your friends as long as they like to prolong their visit. When they intimate an intention to leave you, if you really desire their continuance somewhat longer, frankly say so. Should they, however, have fixed the time, and cannot prolong their stay, facilitate their going by every means in your power; and, while you kindly invite them to renew their visit, point out to them any places of interest on the road, and furnish such information as you possess.

If invited to spend a few days at a friend's house, conform as much as possible to the habits of the family. When parting for the night, inquire respecting the breakfast hour, and ascertain at what time the family meet for prayers. If this right custom prevails, be sure to be in time; and obtain any necessary information from the servant who waits upon you. Give as little trouble as possible; and never think of apologizing for the extra trouble which your visit occasions. Such an apology implies that your friend cannot conveniently entertain you. Your own good sense and delicacy will teach you the desirability of keeping your room tidy, and your articles of dress and toilet as much in order as possible. If there is a deficiency of servants, a lady will certainly not hesitate to make her own bed and to do for herself as much as possible, and for the family all that is in her power.

Few people will leave a friend's house without some expression of regret, and some acknowledgment proffered for the pleasure that has been afforded them.

Conversation.

Let your conversation be adapted as skillfully as possible to your company. Some men make a point of talking commonplace to all ladies alike, as if a woman could only be a trifler. Others, on the contrary, seem to forget in what respects the education of a lady differs from that of a gentleman, and commit the opposite error of conversing on topics with which ladies are seldom acquainted. A lady of sense has as much right to be annoyed by the one as a lady of ordinary education by the other. You cannot pay a finer compliment to a lady of refinement than by leading the conversation into such a channel as may mark your appreciation of her superior attainments.

There is no conversation so graceful, so varied, so sparkling as that of an intellectual and cultivated woman. Excellence on this particular is one of the attributes of the sex, and should be cultivated by every gentlewoman, who aspires to please in general society.

In order to talk well, three conditions are indispensable—tact, a good memory, and a fair education.

Remember that people take more interest in their own affairs than in anything else which you can name. If you wish your conversation to be thoroughly agreeable, lead a mother to talk of her children, a young lady of her last ball, an author of his forthcoming book, or an artist of his exhibition picture. Having furnished the topic, you need only listen; and you are sure to be thought not only agreeable, but thoroughly sensible and well informed.

Be careful, however, on the other hand, not always to make a point of talking to persons upon general matters pertaining to their profession. To show an interest in their immediate concerns is flattering; but to converse with them too much about their own arts looks as if you thought them ignorant of other topics.

Remember in conversation that a voice "gentle and low" is, above all other extraneous acquirements, an excellent thing. There is a certain distinct but subdued tone of voice which is peculiar to only well-bred persons. A loud voice is both disagreeable and vulgar. It is better to err by the use of too low rather than too loud a tone.

Remember that all "slang" is vulgar.

The use of proverbs, and punning, is equally vulgar. Puns, unless they rise to the rank of witticisms, are to be scrupulously avoided.

Long arguments in general company, however entertaining to the disputants, are tiresome to the last degree to all others. You should always endeavor to prevent the conversation from dwelling too long upon one topic.

Religion is a topic which should never be introduced into society. It is the one subject on which persons are most likely to differ, and least able to preserve temper.

Never interrupt a person who is speaking. To listen well is almost as great an art as to talk well. It is not enough *only* to listen. You must endeavor to seem interested in the conversation of others.

It is considered extremely ill bred when two persons whisper in Society, or converse in a language with which all present are not familiar. If you have private matters to discuss, you should appoint a proper time and place to do so, without paying others the ill compliment of-excluding them from your conversation.

If a foreigner be one of the guests at a small party, and does not under stand English sufficiently to follow what is said, good breeding demands that the conversation shall be carried on in his own language. If at a dinner party, the same rule applies to those at his end of the table.

If upon the entrance of a visitor you carry on the thread of a previous conversation, you should briefly recapitulate to him what has been said before he arrived.

Always look, but never stare, at those with whom you converse.

In order to meet the general needs of conversation in society, it is necessary that you should be acquainted with the current news and historical events of at least the last few years.

Never talk upon subjects of which you know nothing, unless it be for the purpose of acquiring information. Many people imagine that because they play a little, sing a little, and frequent exhibitions and operas, they are qualified judges of art. No mistake is more egregious or universal. Those who introduce anecdotes into their conversation are warned that these should invariably be short, witty, eloquent, new, and not far fetched.

Scandal is the least excusable of all conversational vulgarities.

In conversing with people of rank, do not too frequently give them their title.

The great vice of conversation is detraction. Its piquancy is a sad temptation, and all are guilty of it more or less. But it puts you in the light of an envious person, though there may not be a particle of envy present in the matter so far as you are concerned. The presence of envy, real or attributed, will not help you to shine. Speak of the absent as you would if they were present and heard you. Do not say behind a man's back what you would not dare to say to his face. Besides the possible disgrace of having to "eat your own words," it is most unmanly. You can never be wrong in taking a good natured view of the characters of others. It does you no harm; possibly it may do you good. What you say is not so much at the mercy of the company to retail. Good natured remarks, unless maliciously perverted, will stand the saying over again without harm; but ill natured are sure to become harsher in the carrying. Evil speaking is a most unmanly, un-Christian habit, and should be encouraged neither in ourselves nor in others. If a person speaks evil of others to you, be pretty sure that in another company he will speak evil of you. Beware of it not only in yourself, but in others also.

Always be modest in the expression of your sentiments. Do not dogmatically assert, even when you are certain. All appearance of force is sure to be resisted. Be content with the happiness of believing that you are in the right. If your opinions are worth anything at all, they will not only be self-sustaining, but self-comforting also.

Should an argument occur in which you cannot avoid taking a part, remember that he seems to have the best of it that keeps his temper. Feeling more than thought is the tone of company.

Take care you do not touch upon the infirmities or peculiarities of those present. It is difficult enough to convince a man himself of such, but to expose him before the eyes of assembled company is an offence he will never forgive, whether you are right or wrong. Besides, he feels bound to defend himself, and ends with being more confirmed than ever in his eccentricity.

Some people are very fond of "speaking their minds," which, when not under proper restraint, is just another name for being rude. Remember that people are not bound to please you, and the offence that makes you speak your mind may be in yourself and not in them. This is the modest and charitable aspect, and more in consonance with the disposition you ought to have when in company.

Show neither a cringing nor an overbearing spirit. All are upon a level in conversation. He who bears himself over the heads of those whom he deems his inferiors, is the very man to cringe to those whom he deems his superiors. Both are unmanly and impolitic.

Do not spend your power to the utmost. Use it so that you may appear to have more than you spend.

Praise your friends, and leave it to your friends to praise you. It never can come gracefully from yourself.

You need not tell all the truth, but it is absolutely necessary that all you tell be true. Some, however, may have a right to know all the truth. And again, if withholding part of the truth discolor the rest, give it all or none at all.

Despise not another for not possessing talent which you may happen to have. All have not the same talents. He may have one you yourself do not own.

If you risk breaking jests upon others, you must be prepared to have them showered upon yourself.

Do not talk too fast, else you outrun your hearers' understanding. Neither talk too slow, else you fret your hearers into impatience and disgust.

Never let your praise degenerate into flattery. It would only please a fool, and will vitiate your own manliness.

Be not too lavish of your time in company. Men are apt to despise what they can have easily, and to put a value on what is to be had with some difficulty.

If you are desirous of gaining the good opinion of any one, take care how you behave towards him the first time you meet him. First impressions form the seed whence springs his future opinion of you.

Should you find yourself in company which socially may be considered above you, do not show your consciousness of it otherwise than by a modest, dignified reserve. If you are received into the conversation on terms of equality, do not take it as a remarkable condescension. If you are slighted by any one, break off from his converse with you; if you are slighted generally by the company, retire. In both cases the advantage rests with you.

Never set up for a critic. It is simply electing yourself into being a bully of opinion. Those who are weak will fear and hate you; those who are strong will resist and despise you.

Remember that few are capable of judging of talents or genius, but all feel the difference between good and bad behavior.

Do not form your opinion of others from isolated facts. A man may misbehave once and again, and yet be in the main a well behaved person. Remember how often you have forfeited your own esteem, and let your charity cover a multitude of sins in behavior, as in other things.

Unkindly witticism leaves bitterness behind it, that will poison the most genial intercourse.

Learning paraded without judgment and prudence will make you shine as a solemn pedantic fool.

If you are compelled to reprove, do it kindly, so as to convey the least possible offence.

Never volunteer your advice, and even when it is asked give it carefully and cautiously. It is easier to give advice than to follow it, with a prospect of success. He who gives it generally knows not all the special conditions of the case.

Do not hazard crude conjectures regarding results. Things seldom turn out as they are expected. Wise men know this and hold their peace.

Never talk of things in which the company have no interest. They may force attention, but it is sadly at your expense in their estimate of you.

Never trumpet forth your own merit by recounting actions in which you may have gained some credit. It will detract from your desert and from your character as a disinterested and well meaning person.

Do not "pronounce" your sentiments before company. It will make you appear arrogant and self-conceited.

Despise no man's conversation. The meanest may teach you something if you know what is intrinsically good, and if you can approve and appraise it for yourself.

Speak your sentiments in as few words as possible. Tedious conversation is about the most unbearable that can be inflicted on a company. The current of talk ought to be brisk and not sluggish.

If you happen to find yourself on the wrong side of an argument, turn away from it without coming to a conclusion, or say handsomely that you consider yourself wrong. You may often do this without compromising your judgment, as in the case of new facts being presented, or of facts having been falsely represented to you, and now seen in their true light. But never persevere obstinately and fight for your subject as true when you have reason to believe it wrong.

Do not provoke any man. Weapons that cut do not tend to exalt you. Be not easily provoked. The calmer you keep yourself the greater advantage you have over your opponent.

To speak constantly of public characters or distinguished people as your intimate friends, even if they are so, is a certain mark of low-breeding. Boasting of your own position, wealth, luxuries or possession of any kind is in equally bad taste.

Do not ask questions which relate to the private affairs of the person spoken to, and be guarded against conduct which may look like an attempt to force confidence. If too persevering in your inquiries you may be treated, and very properly, as one might treat a highwayman who sought to rob one of any other property. A man's thoughts are certainly his own most private possession, and you must be very intimate to seek to be admitted to a share in them. Even if you are so, it is far

more delicate to wait until confidence is offered to you.   A man has a
perfect right to defend himself from cross-examination by any means,
except positive falsehood.

Do not talk of your high or family connections.   It is absurdly ill
bred, and never heard from people who mix much in the world.   It is
also rude to ask questions about the birth or family of your friends.

There are many who indulge in much flippant talk, and especially at
the dining table.   We have been witness on several occasions to an un-
warrantable amount of this small talk, and were glad to escape therefrom
at the earliest moment possible.   It is true, "a little nonsense now and
then is relished by the wisest man," but for it to take possession of the
hour to the total exclusion of matters of an elevating character is to
make the judicious grieve, and should be frowned upon.

Ladies' Dress.

To dress well requires something more than a full purse and a pretty
figure.   It needs taste, good sense, and refinement.   Dress may also
be classed as one of the fine arts.   It is certainly one of those arts the
cultivation of which is indispensable to any person moving in the upper
or middle classes of society.   Very clever women are too frequently
indifferent to the graces of the toilette; and women who wish to be
thought clever affect indifference.   In the one case it is an error, and in
the other a folly.   It is not enough that a gentlewoman should be clever,
or well educated, or well born.   To take her place in society, she must
be acquainted with all that is herewith taught.   She must, above all
else, know how to enter a room, how to perform a graceful salutation,
and how to dress.   Of these three important qualifications, the most
important, because the most observed, is the latter.

Let your style of dress always be appropriate to the hour of the day.
To dress too finely in the morning, or to be seen in a morning dress in
the evening, is equally vulgar and out of place.   Light and inexpensive
materials are fittest for morning wear; dark silk dresses for the promenade or carriage, and low dresses of rich or transparent stuffs for the
dinner and ball.   A young lady cannot dress with too much simplicity
in the early part of the day.   A morning dress of some simple material,
and delicate white color, with collar and cuffs of spotless linen, is, perhaps, the most becoming and elegant of morning toilettes.

Never dress very richly or showily in the street.   It attracts attention
of no enviable kind, and is looked upon as a want of good breeding.
In the carriage a lady may dress as elegantly as she pleases.   As to ball
room toilettes, its fashions are so variable that it is difficult to pronounce
any permanent rules.   With some diffidence, however, we suggest the
following leading principles: Rich colors harmonize with rich brunette
complexions and dark hair.   Delicate colors are the most suitable for
delicate and fragile styles of beauty.   Very young ladies are never so
suitably attired as in white.   Ladies who dance should wear dresses of

light and diaphanous materials, such as tulle, gauze, crape, etc., over colored silk slips. Silk dresses are not suitable for dancing. A married lady who dances only a few quadrilles may wear a *décolleté* silk dress with propriety.

Very stout persons should never wear white. It has the effect of adding to the bulk of the figure.

Black and scarlet, or black and violet, are worn in mourning.

A lady in deep mourning should not dance at all.

However fashionable it may be to wear very long dresses, those ladies who go to a ball with the intention of dancing, and enjoying the dance, should cause their dresses to be made short enough to clear the ground. Is it not better to accept this slight deviation than to appear for the greater part of an evening in a torn and pinned-up skirt?

Well made shoes, whatever their color or material, and faultless gloves, are indispensable to the effect of a ball room toilette.

Much jewelry is out of place in a ball room. Beautiful flowers, whether natural or artificial, are the loveliest ornaments that a lady can wear on these occasions.

At small dinner parties, low dresses are not so indispensable·as they were held to be some years since. High dresses of transparent materials, and low bodices with capes of black lace, are considered sufficiently full dress on these occasions. At large dinners only the fullest dress is appropriate.

Very young ladies should wear but little jewelry. Pearls are deemed most appropriate for the young and unmarried.

Let your jewelry be always the best of its kind. Nothing is so vulgar, either in youth or in age, as the use of false ornaments. There is as much propriety to be observed in the wearing of jewelry as in the wearing of dresses. Diamonds, pearls, rubies, and all transparent precious stones, belong to evening dress, and should on no account be worn before dinner. In the morning let your rings be of the more simple and massive kind; wear no bracelets, and limit your jewelry to a good brooch, gold chain, and watch. Your diamonds and pearls would be as much out of place during the morning as a low dress, or a wreath.

It is well to remember in the choice of jewelry that mere costliness is not always the test of value; and that an exquisite work of art, such as a fine cameo, or a natural variety, such as black pearl, is a more *distingué* possession than a large brilliant which any rich and tasteless vulgarian can buy as easily as yourself. Of all precious stones, the opal is one of the most lovely and least common-place. No vulgar woman purchases an opal. She invariably prefers the more showy ruby, emerald, or sapphire.

A true gentlewoman is always faultlessly neat. No richness of toilette in the afternoon, no diamonds in the evening, can atone for unbrushed hair, a soiled collar, or untidy slippers at breakfast.

Never be seen in the street without gloves. They should fit to perfection.

In these days of public baths and universal progress, it is unnecessary to more than hint at the necessity of the most fastidious personal cleanliness. The hair, the teeth, the nails, should be faultlessly kept; and a muslin dress that has been worn once too often, a dingy pocket handkerchief, or a soiled pair of light gloves, are things to be scrupulously avoided by any young lady who is ambitious of preserving the exteriors of a gentlewoman.

Remember that the make of your *corsage* is of even greater importance than the make of your dress. No dressmaker can fit you well, or make your bodices in the manner most becoming to your figure, if the *corsage* beneath be not of the best description.

Your shoes and gloves should always be faultless.

Perfumes should be used only in the evening, and then in moderation. Let them be of the most delicate and *recherché* kind. Nothing is more vulgar than a coarse, ordinary scent; and of all coarse, ordinary scents, the most objectionable are musk and patchouli.

A celebrated writer has said that persons habitually attentive to their attire display the same regularity in their domestic affairs. Also that young women who neglect their toilet and manifest little concern about dress, indicate a general disregard of order—a mind ill adapted to the details of house-keeping—a deficiency of taste and of the qualities that inspire love. Hence the desire of exhibiting an amiable exterior is essentially requisite in a young lady, for it indicates cleanliness, sweetness, a love of order and propriety, and all those virtues which are attractive to their associates, and particularly to those of the other sex.

Wherever there is met with a woman whose general style of dress is chaste, elegant and appropriate, she will be found, on further acquaintance, to be, in disposition and mind, an object to admire and love.

Finally, every lady should remember that to dress well is a duty which she owes to society; but that to make it her idol is to commit something worse than a folly. Fashion is made for woman—not woman for fashion.

Gentlemen's Dress.

A gentleman should always be so well dressed that his dress shall never be observed at all. If this sounds enigmatical, it is not so intended. It only implies that perfect simplicity is perfect elegance, and that the true test of taste in the toilet of a gentleman is its entire harmony; unobtrusiveness, and becomingness. If any one should say to you, "What a handsome suit you have on!" you may depend that a less handsome one be in better taste. If you hear it said that Mr. So-and-So wears superb jewelry, you may conclude that he wears too much. Display is ever to be avoided, especially in matters of dress. The toilet is the domain of the fair sex. Let a wise man leave its graces and luxuries to his wife, daughters or sisters, and seek to be himself appreciated for something of higher worth than the stud in his shirt or the trinkets on his chain.

To be too much in the fashion is as vulgar as to be too far behind it. No really well bred man follows every new cut that he sees in his tailor's fashion book.

In the morning wear frock coats, double breasted waistcoats, and trousers of light or dark colors, according to the season.

In the evening, though only in the bosom of your own family, wear only black, and be as scrupulous to put on a dress coat as if you expected visitors. If you have sons, bring them up to do the same. It is the observance of these minor trifles in domestic etiquette which marks the true gentleman.

For evening parties, dinner parties, and balls, wear a black dress coat, black trousers, black silk or cloth waistcoat, white cravat, white or gray kid gloves, and thin patent leather boots. A black cravat may be worn in full dress, but is not so elegant as a white one.

Let your jewelry be of the best, but the least gaudy description, and wear it very sparingly. A single stud, a gold watch and guard, and one handsome ring are as many ornaments as a gentleman can wear with propriety. As to the choice of jewelry much that we have said concerning ladies' dress will apply equally to gentlemen.

Unless you are a snuff taker never carry any but a white pocket-handkerchief.

If in the morning you wear a long cravat fastened by a pin, be careful to avoid what may be called alliteration of color. A turqoise pin in a violet colored cravat produces a frightful effect. Choose, if possible, complementary colors, and then secondaries. For instance, if the stone in your pin be a turquoise wear it with brown, or crimson mixed with black, or black and orange. If a ruby, contrast it with shades of green. The same rule holds good with regard to the mixture and contrast of colors in your waistcoat and cravat. Thus, a buff waist-coat and a blue tie, or brown and blue, or brown and green, or brown and magenta, green and magenta, green and mauve, are all good arrangements of color.

Colored shirts may be worn in the morning, but they should be small in pattern and quiet in color.

As "cleanliness is next to godliness," it should be fastidiously observed as to the hair, teeth, nails and general dress, and thus preserve the exterior of a gentleman.

Morning and Evening Parties.

The morning party is a modern invention. It was unknown to our fathers and mothers, and even to ourselves until recent years. A morning party is given during the months of June, July, August, September, and sometimes October. It begins about two o'clock and ends about seven, and the entertainment consists for the most part of conversation, music, and (if there be a garden) croquet, lawn tennis, archery, etc. The refreshments are given in the form of a *déjeûner à la fourchette*. Receptions are held during the Winter season.

Elegant morning dress, general good manners, and some acquaintance with the topics of the day and the games above named, are all the qualifications especially necessary to a lady or gentleman at a morning party, and "At Homes;" music and elocution at receptions.

An evening party begins about nine o'clock p. m., and ends about midnight, or somewhat later. Good breeding neither demands that you should present yourself at the commencement nor remain till the close of the evening, you come and go as may be most convenient to you, and by these means are at liberty, during the height of the season when evening parties are numerous, to present yourself at two or three houses during a single evening.

When your name is announced, look for the lady of the house, and pay your respects to her before you even seem to see any other of your friends who may be in the room. At very large and fashionable receptions the hostess is generally to be found near the door. Should you, however, find yourself separated by a dense crowd of guests, you are at liberty to recognize those who are near you and those whom you encounter as you make your way slowly through the throng.

If you are at the house of a new acquaintance and find yourself among entire strangers, remember that by so meeting under one roof you are all in a certain sense made known to one another, and should, therefore, converse freely, as equals. To shrink away to a side table and affect to be absorbed in some album or illustrated work; or, if you find one unlucky acquaintance in the room to fasten upon her or him like a drowning man clinging to a spar, are gaucheries which no shyness can excuse. An easy and unembarrassed manner, and the self possession requisite to open a conversation with those who happen to be near you are the indispensable credentials of all well bred people.

If you possess any musical accomplishments, do not wait to be pressed and entreated by your hostess, but comply immediately when she pays you the compliment of inviting you to play or sing. Remember, however, that only the lady of the house has the right to ask you. If others do so, you can put them off in some polite way, but must not comply till the hostess herself invites you.

Be scrupulous to observe silence when any of the company are playing or singing. Remember that they are doing this for the amusement of the rest; and that to talk at such a time is as ill bred as if you were to turn your back upon a person who was talking to you and begin a conversation with some one else.

If you are yourself the performer, bear in mind that in music, as in speech, "brevity is the soul of wit." Two verses of a song, or four pages of a piece, are at all times enough to give pleasure. If your audience desire more they will ask for it; and it is infinitely more flattering to be encored than to receive the thanks of your hearers, not so much in gratitude for what you have given them, but in relief that you have left off. You should try to suit your music, like your conversation, to your company. A solo of Beethoven's would be as much out of place in some circles as a comic song at a Quakers' meeting. To those who only care for the light popularities of the season, give Verdi, Suppé, Sullivan, or Offenbach. To connoisseurs, if you perform well enough to venture, give such music as will be likely to meet the exigencies of a fine taste. Above all, attempt nothing that you cannot execute with ease and precision.

If the party be of a small and social kind and those games called by the French *les jeux innocents* are proposed, do not object to join in them when invited. It may be that they demand some slight exercise of wit and readiness, and that you do not feel yourself calculated to shine in them; but it is better to seem dull than disagreeable, and those who are obliging can always find some clever neighbor to assist them in the moment of need. The game of "consequences" is one which unfortunately gives too much scope to liberty of expression. If you join in this game, we cannot too earnestly enjoin you never to write down one word which the most pure minded woman present might not read aloud without a blush. Jests of an equivocal character are not only vulgar but contemptible.

Impromptu charades are frequently organized at friendly parties. Unless you have really some talent for acting and some readiness of speech, you should remember that you only put others out and expose your own inability by taking part in these entertainments. Of course, if your help is really needed, and you would disoblige by refusing, you must do your best and by doing it as quietly and coolly as possible, avoid being awkward or ridiculous.

Even though you may take no pleasure in cards, some knowledge of the etiquette and rules belonging to the games most in vogue is necessary to you in society. If a fourth hand is wanted at euchre, or if the rest of the company sit down to a round game, you would be deemed guilty of an impoliteness if you refused to join.

The games most commonly played in society are euchre, draw-poker, and whist.

Never let even politeness induce you to play for high stakes. Etiquette is the minor morality of life, but it never should be allowed to outweigh the higher code of right and wrong.

If you have occasion to use your handkerchief, do so as noiselessly as possible. To blow your nose as if it were a trombone, or to turn your head aside when using your handkerchief, are vulgarities scrupulously to be avoided.

Never stand upon the hearth with your back to the fire or stove, either in a friend's house or your own.

Never offer any one the chair from which you have just risen, unless there be no other disengaged.

If, when supper is announced, no lady has been specially placed under your care by the hostess, offer your arm to whichever lady you may have last conversed with.

Should an impromptu polka or quadrille be got up after supper at a party where no dancing was intended, be sure not to omit putting on gloves before you stand up. It is well always to have a pair of white gloves in your pocket in case of need; but even black are better under these circumstances than none.

In retiring from a crowded party it is unnecessary that you should seek out the hostess for the purpose of bidding her a formal good night.

By doing this you would, perhaps, remind others that it was getting late, and cause the party to break up. If you meet the lady of the house on your way to the drawing room door, take your leave of her as unobtrusively as possible, and slip away without attracting the attention of her other guests.

Carefully avoid all peculiarities of manner, and every wish to show off or to absorb conversation to yourself. Be also very careful not to appear to be wiser than the company. If a fact in history is mentioned, even if it be not quite correct, do not set the narrator right, unless in a very delicate and submissive manner. If an engraving of distant scenery or foreign buildings is shown, do not industriously point out inaccuracies. It may be that such occur, but finding fault is never acceptable; it conveys a censure on the taste or information of the possessor; or it suggests that he has been imposed upon—an idea which is always productive of mortification. Such attempts to appear wiser than the rest of the company, interfere with the pleasure of the party, and the person who falls into them is never long acceptable.

There is a custom which is sometimes practiced both in the assembly room and at private parties, which cannot be too strongly reprehended; we allude to the habit of ridicule and ungenerous criticism of those who are ungraceful or otherwise obnoxious to censure, which is indulged in by the thoughtless, particularly among the dancers. Of its gross impropriety and vulgarity we need hardly express an opinion; but there is such an utter disregard for the feelings of others implied in this kind of negative censorship, that we cannot forbear to warn our young readers to avoid it. The "Koran" says: "Do not mock—the mocked may be better than the mocker." Those you condemn may not have had the same advantages as yourself in acquiring grace or dignity, while they may be infinitely superior in purity of heart and mental accomplishments. The advice of Chesterfield to his son, in his commerce with society, to do as you would be done by, is founded on the Christian precept, and worthy of commendation. Imagine yourself the victim of another's ridicule, and you will cease to indulge in a pastime which only gains for you the hatred of those you satirize, if they chance to observe you and the contempt of others who have noticed your violation of politeness, and abuse of true sociality.

The Dinner Party.

To be acquainted with every detail of the etiquette pertaining to this subject is of the highest importance. Ease, *savoir faire*, and good breeding are nowhere more indispensable than at the dinner table, and the absence of them is nowhere more apparent. How to eat soup and what to do with a cherry stone are weighty considerations when taken as the index of social status; and it is not too much to say that one who elected to take claret with fish, or ate peas with a knife would justly risk the punishment of being banished from good society.

An invitation to dine should be replied to immediately, and unequivocally accepted or declined. Once accepted, nothing but an event of the last importance should cause you to fail in your engagement.

To be exactly punctual is the strictest politeness on these occasions. If you are too early, you are in the way; if too late you spoil the dinner, annoy the hostess, and are hated by the rest of the guests. Some authorities are even of opinion that in the question of a dinner party "never" is better than "late"; and one author has gone so far as to say, "if you do not reach the house till dinner is served, you had better retire, and send an apology, and not interrupt the harmony of the courses by awkward excuses and cold acceptance."

When the party is assembled, the mistress or master of the house will point out to each gentleman the lady whom he is to conduct to the table. The lady who is the greatest stranger should be taken by the master of the house, and the gentleman who is the greatest stranger should conduct the hostess. Married ladies take precedence of single ladies, elder ladies of younger ones, and so forth.

When dinner is announced, the host offers his arm to the lady of most distinction, invites the rest to follow by a few words or a bow, and leads the way. The lady of the house should then follow with the gentleman who is most entitled to that honor, and the visitors follow in the order that has been previously arranged. The lady of the house, however, frequently remains till the last, that she may see her guests go in their prescribed order, but the plan is not a convenient one. It is much better that the hostess should be in her place as the guests enter the dining room, in order that she may indicate their seats to them as they enter, and not find them all crowded together in uncertainty when she arrives. The plan of cards, with the names of the guests on them, opposite their chairs, is a very useful one.

The number of guests at a dinner party should always be determined by the size of the table. When the party is too small, conversation flags, and a general air of desolation pervades the table. When they are too many, every one is inconvenienced. A space of two feet should be allowed to each person. It is well to arrange a party in such wise that the number of ladies and gentlemen be equal.

The lady of the house takes the head of the table. The gentleman who led her to dinner occupies the seat on her right hand and the gentleman next in order of precedence that on her left. The master of the house takes the foot of the table. The lady whom he escorted sits on his right hand and the lady next in order of precedence on his left.

The gentlemen who support the lady of the house should offer to relieve her of the duties of hostess. Many ladies are well pleased thus to delegate the difficulties of carving, and all gentlemen who accept invitations to dinner should be prepared to render such assistance when called upon. To offer to carve a dish and then perform the office unskilfully is an unpardonable *gaucherie*. Every gentleman should carve, and carve well.

As soon as you are seated at table, remove your gloves, place your table napkin across your knees, and remove the roll which you will probably find within it to the left side of your plate.

The soup should be placed on the table first. All well ordered dinners begin with soup, whether in Summer or Winter. The lady of the house should help it, and send it round without asking each individual in turn. It is as much an understood thing as the bread beside each plate, and those who do not choose it are always at liberty to leave it untasted.

In eating soup, remember always to take it from the side of the spoon, and to make no sound in doing so.

If the servants do not go round with wine, the gentlemen should help the ladies and themselves to sherry or sauterne immediately after the soup.

You should never ask for a second supply of soup or fish; it delays the next course and keeps the table waiting.

Never offer to "assist" your neighbors to this or that dish. The word is inexpressibly vulgar—all the more vulgar for its affectation of elegance "Shall I send you some mutton?" or "may I help you to canvas back?" is better chosen and better bred.

As a general rule it is better not to ask your guests if they will partake of the dishes, but to send the plates round, and let them accept or decline as they please. At very large dinners it is sometimes customary to distribute little lists of the order of the dishes at intervals along the table Of course this gives somewhat the air of a dinner at a hotel, but it has the advantage of enabling the visitors to select their fare, and, as "forewarned is forearmed," to keep a corner, as the children say, for their favorite dishes.

If you are asked to take wine, it is polite to select the same as that which your interlocutor is drinking. If you invite a lady to take wine. you should ask her which she will prefer, and then take the same your-self. Should you, however, for any reason prefer some other vintage, you can take it by courteously requesting her permission.

As soon as you are helped, begin to eat; or, if the viands are too hot for your palate, take up your knife and fork and appear to begin. To wait for others is now not only old fashioned but ill bred.

Never offer to pass on the plate to which you have been helped.

In helping soup, fish, or any other dish, remember that to overfill a plate is as bad as to supply it too scantily.

Silver fish knives will now always be met with at the best tables; but where there are none, a piece of crust should be taken in the left hand and the fork in the right. There is no exception to this rule in eating fish.

It is scarcely necessary to remind you that you should never, under any circumstances, convey a knife to the mouth. Peas are eaten with the fork; tarts, curry, and puddings of all kinds with the spoon.

Always help fish with a fish slice, and tart and puddings with the spoon, or, if necessary, a spoon and fork.

Asparagus must be helped with the asparagus tongs.

In eating asparagus, it is well to observe what others do, and act accordingly. Some very well bred people eat it with the fingers; others cut off the heads and convey them to the mouth upon the fork. In eating stone fruit, such as cherries, damsons, etc., the same rule had better be observed. Some put the stones out from the mouth into a spoon, and so convey them to the plate. Others cover the mouth with the hand, drop them unseen into the palm, and so deposit them on the side of the plate. The latter is the best way, as it effectually conceals the return of the stones, which is certainly the point of highest importance. Of one be sure—never drop them from the mouth to the plate.

In helping sauce, always pour it on the side of the plate.

If the servants do not go round with the wine (which is by far the best custom), the gentlemen at a dinner table should take upon themselves the office of helping those ladies who sit near them. Ladies cannot very well ask for wine, but they can always decline it. At all events they do not like to be neglected, or to see gentlemen liberally helping themselves, without observing whether their fair neighbors' glasses are full or empty.

Unless you are a total abstainer, it is extremely uncivil to decline taking wine if you are invited to do so. In accepting you have only to pour a little fresh wine into your glass, look at the person who invited you, bow slightly, and take a sip from the glass. It is particularly ill bred to empty your glass on these occasions.

Certain wines are taken with certain dishes, by old established custom —as sherry or sauterne with soup and fish; hock and claret with roast meat; punch with turtle; champagne with sweetbread or cutlets; port with venison; port or burgundy with game; sparkling wines between the roast and the confectionery; madeira with sweets; port with cheese; and for dessert, port, tokay, madeira, sherry, and claret. Red wines should never be iced, even in summer. Claret and burgundy should always be slightly warmed; claret cup and champagne should, of course, be iced.

Instead of cooling their wines in the ice pail, some hosts introduce clear ice upon the table, broken in small lumps, to be put inside the glasses. This cannot be too strictly reprehended. Melting ice weakens the quality and flavor of the wine. Those who desire to drink wine and water can ask for iced water if they choose; but it savors too much of economy on the part of a host to insinuate the ice inside the glasses of his guests when the wine could be more effectually iced outside the bottle.

A silver knife and fork should be placed to each guest at dessert.

If you are asked to prepare fruit for a lady, be careful to do so by means of the silver knife and fork only, and never to touch it with your fingers.

It is wise never to partake of any dish without knowing of what ingredients it is composed. You can always ask the servant who hands it to you, and you thereby avoid all danger of having to commit the impoliteness of leaving it, and showing that you do not approve of it.

Never speak while you have anything in your mouth.

Be careful never to taste soups or puddings till you are sure they are sufficiently cool; as, by disregarding this caution, you may be compelled to swallow what is dangerously hot or be driven to the unpardonable alternative of returning it to your plate.

When eating or drinking, avoid every kind of audible testimony to the fact.

Finger glasses, containing water slightly warmed and perfumed, are placed to each person at dessert. In these you may dip the tips of your fingers, wiping them afterwards on your table napkin. If the finger glass and doiley are placed on your dessert plate, you should immediately remove the doiley to the left of your plate and place the finger glass upon it. By these means you leave the right for the wine glasses.

Be careful to know the shapes of the various kinds of wine glasses commonly in use, in order that you may never put forward one for another. High and narrow, and very broad and shallow glasses, are used for champagne; large goblet shaped glasses for burgundy and claret; ordinary wine glasses for sherry and madeira; green glasses for hock, and somewhat large, bell shaped glasses for port.

Port, sherry and madeira are decanted. Hocks and champagnes appear in their native bottles. Claret and burgundy are handed round in a claret jug.

The servants leave the room when the dessert is on the table.

Coffee and liquors should be handed round when the dessert has been about a quarter of an hour on the table. After this the ladies generally retire.

When the ladies are leaving the dining room, the gentlemen should all rise in their places, and not resume their seats until the last lady is gone.

If you should unfortunately overturn or break anything, do not apologize for it. You can show your regret in your face, but it is not well bred to put it into words.

To abstain from taking the last piece on the dish, or the last glass of wine in the decanter, only because it is the last, is highly ill bread. It implies a fear on your part that the vacancy cannot be supplied, and almost conveys an affront to your host.

A dinner, to be excellent, need not consist of a great variety of dishes, but everything should be of the best and the cookery perfect. That which should be cool should be as cool as ice; that which should be hot should be smoking; the attendance should be rapid and noiseless: the guests well assorted; the wines of the best quality; the host attentive and courteous; the room well lighted and the time punctual.

Never reprove or give directions to your servants before guests. If a dish is not placed precisely where you would have wished it to stand, or the order of a course is reversed, let the error pass unobserved by yourself, and you may depend it will be unnoticed by others.

The duties of hostess at a dinner party are not onerous, but they demand tact and good breeding, grace of bearing, and self-posession of no ordinary degree. She does not often carve. She has no active duties to perform, but she must neglect nothing, forget nothing, put all her guests at their ease, encourage the timid, draw out the silent, and pay every possible attention to the requirements of each and all around her. No accident must ruffle her temper. No disappointment must embarrass her. She must see her old china broken without a sigh, and her best glass shattered with a smile.

To sit long in the dining room after the ladies have retired is to pay a bad compliment to the hostess and her fair visitors; and it is still worse to rejoin them with a flushed face and impaired power of thought. A refined gentleman is always temperate.

Some persons, in helping their guests, or recommending dishes to their taste, preface every such action with a eulogy on its merits, and draw every bottle of wine with an account of its virtues; others, running into the contrary extreme, regret or fear that each dish is not exactly as it should be; that the cook, etc., etc. Both of these habits are grievous errors. You should leave it to your guests alone to approve, or suffer one of your intimate friends who is present, to vaunt your wine.

It is not good taste to praise extravagantly every dish that is set before you; but if there are some things that are really very nice, it is well to speak in their praise. But, above all things, avoid seeming indifferent to the dinner that is provided for you, as that might be construed into a dissatisfaction with it.

Unless you are requested to do so, never select any particular part of a dish; but if your host asks you what part you prefer, name some part, as in this case the incivility would consist in making your host choose as well as carve for you.

Politeness demands that you remain at least an hour in the parlor, after dinner; and, if you can dispose of an entire evening, it would be well to devote it to the person who has entertained you. It is excessively rude to leave the house as soon as dinner is over.

Table Talk.

This is a sphere in which the most distinguished have endeavored to shine. Volumes of their table talk have been published, and this aphoristic literature is held in high esteem. While the dinner is being served the prelude to the conversation is being carried on. Now is the favorable time for gaining a knowledge of the different individuals with whom you are to pass the next few hours. At this period the tone of conversation is not very high pitched. The topics are generally of a commonplace kind, for as yet you have had no common ground on which to meet your associates. The general news of the day, the interchange of civilities, public amusements—these form a starting point. The association of ideas and their interchange keep up the flow. Gradually mind discloses itself to mind, and the mere talk passes into genuine conversation. The commonplace topics enable us to form an estimate of the company—to distinguish the talkative from the taciturn, the quick from the dull, the cheerful, jovial man from the slow and the sour.

2

If you desire to shine to advantage at dinner, order and husband your topics like the courses that come before you, for a great deal depends on the inclination of your associates to listen to you. Let them be light at first and more substantial as you proceed, and if you have wit, spend it judiciously in seasoning all.

During the soup course, conversation is almost entirely dispensed with. The minds of all are generally engrossed with one topic, and to talk upon that topic is forbidden by the laws of dinner etiquette. The animal appetite must be silenced before the rational faculty is allowed to play.

After the first course, you may begin to feel the pulse of your neighbor, or *vis-à-vis*, by some little approach to gayety, but beware of attracting general attention. At the second course the appetite begins to abate, and a restraining pause ensues. Now they like nothing better than to talk and listen for a short time. This is the time for the interchange of pleasantries, and short lively anecdotes. But don't bother the mind with any serious work to do, for it is still under the sway of the stomach, and will not brook anything that requires sustained attention. People. resent anything that looks like an attempt to spoil their dinner or the digestion of it.

As the courses proceed you may open out more freely, for all are becoming emancipated from the dominion of physical appetite, and the mental is now decidedly in the ascendant. Beware still, however, of boring your neighbors with too heavy talk, or too continuous, for the reign of free uninterrupted conversation has not yet begun.

But when the desert is on the table—when the ripe delicate fruit is set, and the sparkling wines stream from the crystal, then let flow your raciest thoughts—your wit—your humor—your fancies—whatever you may excel in. No restraint is needed now but that of good sense, sound judgment and manly courtesy.

Visiting at a Friend's House.

A visitor is bound by the laws of social intercourse to conform in all respects to the habits of the house. In order to do this effectually, inquiry should be made as to what those habits are. To keep your friend's breakfast on the table till a late hour; to delay the dinner by want of punctuality; to accept other invitations, and treat his house as if it were merely a place to sleep in; or to keep the family up till unwonted hours, are alike evidences of a want of good feeling and good breeding.

At breakfast and lunch absolute punctuality is not imperative; but a visitor should avoid being always the last to appear at table.

No order of precedence is observed at either breakfast or luncheon. Persons take their seats as they come in, and, having exchanged their morning salutations, begin to eat without waiting for the rest of the party.

If letters are delivered to you at breakfast or luncheon, you may read them by asking permission from the lady who presides at the urn.

Always hold yourself at the disposal of those in whose house you are visiting. If they propose to ride, drive, walk, or otherwise occupy the day, you may take it for granted that these plans are made with reference to your enjoyment. You should, therefore, receive them with cheerfulness, enter into them with alacrity, and do your best to seem pleased, and be pleased, by the efforts which your friends make to entertain you.

You should never take a book from the library to your own room without requesting permission to borrow it. When it is lent, you should take every care that it sustains no injury while in your possession.

A guest should endeavor to amuse oneself as much as possible, and not be continually dependent on the hosts for entertainment. They should remember that, however welcome they may be, they are not always wanted.

A visitor should avoid giving unnecessary trouble to the servants of the house.

The signal for retiring to rest is generally given by the appearance of the servant with wine, water and biscuits, where a late dinner hour is observed and suppers are not the custom. This is the last refreshment of the evening, and the visitor will do well to rise and wish good night shortly after it has been partaken of by the family.

On the Promenade.

It is a gentleman's and lady's duty to be polite in all places. Unless parties have done something to forfeit the respect dictated by the common rules of politeness, there should be no deviation from this practice. And this politeness should be observed on the promenade as well as elsewhere.

It has been said that "a bow is a note drawn at sight." You are bound to acknowledge it immediately, and to the full amount.

The hat should be quite lifted from the head. On meeting friends with whom you are likely to shake hands, remove your hat with the left hand in order to leave the right hand free.

If you meet a lady in the street whom you are sufficiently intimate to address, do not stop her, but turn round and walk beside her in whichever direction she is going. When you have said all that you wish to say you can take your leave.

If you meet a lady with whom you are not particularly well acquainted, wait for her recognition before you venture to bow to her.

In bowing to a lady whom you are not going to address, lift your hat with that hand which is farthest from her. If you pass her on the right side, use your left hand; if on the left, use your right.

If you are on horseback and wish to converse with a lady who is on foot, you should dismount and lead your horse, so as not to give her the fatigue of looking up to your level. Neither should you subject her to the impropriety of carrying on a conversation in a tone necessarily louder than is sanctioned by the laws of good breeding.

When meeting friends or acquaintances in the streets, at exhibitions, or any public places, take care not to pronounce their names so loudly as to attract the attention of the passers by. Never call across the street. Never carry on a dialogue in a public vehicle, unless your interlocutor occupies the seat beside your own.

In walking with a lady, take charge of any parcel or book with which she may be encumbered.

You should offer your arm to a lady with whom you are walking whenever her safety, comfort, or convenience may seem to require such attention on your part. At night your arm should always be tendered, and also when ascending the steps of a public building. In walking with any person you should keep step with military precision, and with ladies and elderly people you should always accommodate your speed to theirs.

If a lady with whom you are walking receives the salute of a person who is a stranger to you, you should return it, not for yourself, but for her.

When you are passing in the street, and see coming toward you a person of your acquaintance, whether a lady or an elderly person, you should offer them the wall, that is to say, the side next the houses. If a carriage should happen to stop in such a manner as to leave only a narrow passage between it and the houses, beware of elbowing and rudely crowding the passengers, with a view to get by more expeditiously; wait your turn, and if any of the persons before mentioned come up, you should edge up to the wall, in order to give them the place. They also as they pass, should bow politely to you.

If a lady addresses an inquiry to a gentleman on the street. he will lift his hat, or at least touch it respectfully, as he replies. If he cannot give the information required, he will express his regrets.

When tripping over the pavement, a lady should gracefully raise her dress a little above her ankle. With her right hand she should hold together the folds of her gown and draw them towards the right side. To raise the dress on both sides, and with both hands is vulgar. This ungraceful practice can be tolerated only for a moment when the mud is very deep.

Most American ladies in our cities wear too rich and expensive dresses in the street. Some, indeed, will sweep the side-walks with costly stuffs only fit for a drawing-room or a carriage This is in bad taste, and is what illnatured people would term snobbish.

If a gentleman is walking with two ladies in a rain-storm. and there is but one umbrella, he should give it to his companions and walk outside. Nothing can be more absurd than to see a gentleman walking between two ladies holding an umbrella, which perfectly protects himself. and sends little streams of water from every point on the dresses of the ladies he is supposed to be sheltering.

If a lady is caught in a shower, and a gentleman offers an umbrella, she may accept it, if he is going in the same direction as herself and accompanies her. If not, and he still insists, etiquette requires the return of the umbrella as soon as the lady reaches her destination. No lady may accept this courtesy from a strange gentleman, but must decline it firmly, but politely.

If a gentleman meets a lady friend who is walking with any one he does not know, he must not stop, nor must he stop if his companion is unacquainted with a lady friend whom he may chance to meet. The lady, however, has a perfect right to do as she likes. If she should stop, the strangers must be introduced, and none of the group should go on and wait, whether the introduction be agreeable or not.

A lady should avoid walking very rapidly. It is very ungraceful and unbecoming.

Swinging the arms is an awkward and ill-bred habit.

If occasion demands your remaining stationary upon the steps or in the portico of a public edifice, make room at once for ladies who may be entering, and avoid any appearance of curiosity regarding them. This has become the more necessary of late years, owing to the too frequent rudeness of men in stationing themselves at the entrances of churches,. concert-rooms, opera-houses, etc., for the express purpose, apparently, of staring every modest woman who may chance to enter out of countenance. No one possessed of true good-breeding will indulge in a practice so at variance with propriety. A similar course should be pursued when occupying a place upon the steps, or at the windows of an hotel or public building. Carefully avoid all semblance of staring at ladies passing in the street, alighting from a carriage, etc., and make no comment, even of a complimentary nature, in a voice that can possible reach their ears. So when walking in the street, if beauty or grace attract your attention, let your regard be respectful, and even then not too fixed. An audible comment or exclamation addressed to a companion, a laugh, a familiar stare, are each and all, when any stranger and more especially a lady, I the subject of them, unhandsome in the extreme.

Should ladies whom you know be observed, unattended by a gentleman, alighting from or entering a cab or carriage, especially if there is no footman and the driver maintains his seat, at once advance, hold the door open and offer your hand, or protect a dress from the wheel. and bowing pass on, all needed service rendered, or if more familiarity and your own wish sanction it, accompany them where they may be about to enter. In attending them into a shop always give them precedence, holding the door open from without if practicable.

Shopping.

Etiquette is too often disregarded in that grand aim of most ladies' excursions on the street—shopping. The clerks and salesmen, both male and female, and the driver in large retail emporiums, experience sufficient trices which may not be avoided, without having them added to by rude and impolite people. True politeness will lead a lady to pay some attention to their feelings, and they are quick to observe who are ladylike and who are not, in their intercourse with them.

Do not enter a store unless you have some errand. Ask for what you want as explicitly as possible, and do not take the time of the attendants by examining fifty things that you do not want.

If you do not intend to purchase goods, but wish to examine them for future selection, say so.

Never try to cheapen goods. If the price is too high for the quality offered, or will not suit your purse, look elsewhere for what will better suit you.

Never keep a clerk waiting while you chat with a friend. If you desire to speak with your acquaintances, stand aside, that the clerk may understand he is released for the time, and free to wait upon other customers.

Never call away a clerk who is waiting upon some one else. Wait, if you have business with an especial clerk, until you see that he is disengaged.

Sneering remarks upon goods is rude in the extreme. If they do not suit you, you are not obliged to buy them; but spare your comments.

Lounging over a counter is ill-bred.

Putting your elbows on a counter is rude.

Pushing aside another person is an act of ill-breeding.

Be careful not to injure goods by handling.

Never ask for patterns without apologizing for the trouble, and not then unless you really intend to return for the goods, as when you are shopping for a friend, or wish for the judgment or taste of another person.

Never take hold of a piece of goods another person is examining. Wait until it is replaced upon the counter, when you are at liberty to take it up.

It is extremely rude to interrupt friends you may meet in a store, to ask their attention to your purchase, before they have finished their own. It is as rude to offer your opinion, unasked, upon their judgment or taste in selection of goods.

Riding and Driving.

In riding, as in walking, give the lady the wall.

If you assist a lady to mount, hold your hand at a convenient distance from the ground that she may put her foot in it. As she springs, you aid her by the impetus of your hand. In doing this, it is always better to agree upon a signal, that her spring and your assistance may come at the same moment.

When the lady is in the saddle it is your place to find the stirrup for her and guide her left foot to it. When this is done she rises in her seat and you assist her to draw her habit straight.

If the lady be light, you must be careful not to give her too much impetus in mounting. There have been many occasions where the lady has been nearly thrown over her horse by a misplaced zeal of this kind.

In riding with two ladies, if both are good horsewomen, the gentleman should ride to the right of both; but if they are inexperienced, it is better for him to ride between them, to be ready to assist them if necessary.

A gentleman must never touch a lady's horse unless she actually requires his aid; but he should be very watchful and ready for the most prompt attention if it is needed.

If a gentleman on horseback meet a lady who is walking, and stops to speak to her, he must dismount until she bows and leaves him.

A gentleman must go forward whenever a gate is to be opened or an obstruction to be removed, and clear the way for the lady; he must leap first when there is a fence or ditch to be crossed; he must pay all tolls; must first test any dangerous-looking place and must try to select the most desirable roads.

In dismounting, a gentleman must offer a lady his right hand, taking her left, and using his own left as a step for her foot, declining it gently as soon as she rises from the saddle, and before she springs. To spring from the saddle is not only awkward, but dangerous, and will often confuse a gentleman who is accustomed only to the proper mode of assisting the ladies to whom he offers his services as escort.

No gentleman will force a lady to ride faster than she may find agreeable, by an endeavor to display his own horsemanship.

A gentleman must be careful to protect his lady companion from the dust and mud, as far as possible; and if there is a choice of side for shade, he may, with propriety, ride upon her left, or fall a little behind her, to allow her to take advantage of it.

In riding with an elderly gentleman, a younger man should extend all the courtesies of the road, the shady side, the choice of speed, the choice also of direction, and, if there be a difference, the best horse.

In a carriage, where a coachman is outside, the seat on the right hand, facing the horses, is the seat of honor, and should be given to a lady, an elderly gentleman, or the guest.

When the carriage stops, the gentleman should alight first in order to assist the lady.

To get in and out of a carriage gracefully is a simple but important accomplishment. If there is but one step, and you are going to take your seat facing the horses, put your left foot on the step, and enter the carriage with your right in such a manner as to drop at once into your seat. If you are to sit with your back to the horses, reverse the process. As you step into the carriage, be careful to keep your back towards the seat you are about to occupy, so as to avoid the awkwardness of turning when you are once in.

A gentleman cannot be too careful to avoid stepping on ladies' dresses when he gets in or out of a carriage. He should also avoid shutting them in with the door.

When a gentleman is about to take a lady, an older gentleman, or a guest to drive, he must drive as close as possible to the mounting block or curb, head his horse towards the middle of the road, and back his buggy or wagon slightly, separating the fore and hind wheels as much as possible. This is especially necessary when a lady is to ascend to the wagon, as it gives space for her dress to avoid the contact of the wheels, and allows room for the driver to tuck her dress in after she is seated. It is best to have always a carriage-blanket to cover entirely the skirt of a lady's dress, that the mud of the road may not splash it.

When there is a post, it is always safest to hitch the horse securely, and give both hands to the lady's service. Never allow the horse to stand without some hold upon him; if there is no post, the reins must be held firmly in one hand, while the other assists the lady.

No gentleman will show off his driving, if he finds his companion timid. He will adopt the pace most agreeable to her, even if it condemns him to a funeral slowness.

It is courtesy for the owner of a wagon, when driving a gentleman friend, to offer him the reins, but the offer should never be accepted. If, when driving a long distance, with a hard-mouthed horse, the companion can really relieve a tired driver, it is then both courteous and kind to offer to take the reins for a time; but it is not etiquette so to offer under any other circumstances.

If you offer a seat in a private carriage to any friends you may meet whilst abroad, you must accompany them to their destination, no matter how far it may be out of your own way.

For a gentleman, when driving with a lady, to put his arm across the back of the seat, around her, is a piece of impertinence which any well-bred lady will very justly resent.

If offered a seat in the carriage of a gentleman friend, you should motion him to be seated first; but if he stands aside for you, bow, and precede him.

After assisting a lady to her seat, be certain that her parasol, shawl, and fan are all conveniently placed for her use before you take your own seat. Allow her all the space you can, and be especially careful that the motion of your arms does not incommode her.

Party and Ball Room Etiquette.

The number of invitations to a ball should be limited by the proportions of the dancing or ball room. A prudent hostess will always invite a few more guests than she really desires to entertain, in the certainty that there will be some desertions when the appointed evening comes round; but she will at the same time remember that to overcrowd her room is to spoil the pleasure of those who love dancing, and that a party of this kind when too numerously attended is as great a failure as one at which too few are present.

A room which is nearly square, yet a little longer than it is broad, will be found the most favorable for a ball. It admits of two quadrille parties, or two round dances, at the same time. In a perfectly square room, this arrangement is not so practicable or pleasant. A very long and narrow room is of the worst shape for the purpose of dancing, and is fit only for quadrilles and country dances.

The top of the ball room is the part nearest the musicians, and is generally at the farthest point from the door. Dancers should be careful to ascertain the top of the room before taking their places, as the top couples always lead the dances.

A good floor is of the first importance. In a private house nothing can be better than a smooth, well stretched holland, with the carpet underneath.

Abundance of light and free ventilation are indispensable to the spirits and comforts of the guests and dancers.

Good music is a very necessary adjunct to the prosperity of a ball. No hostess should tax her friends for this part of the entertainment. It is the most injurious economy imaginable. Ladies who would prefer to dance are tied to the pianoforte; and as few amateurs have been trained in the art of playing dance music, with that strict attention to time and accent which is absolutely necessary to the comfort of the dancers, a total and general discontent is sure to be the result. To play dance music thoroughly well is a branch of the art which requires considerable practice. Those who give private balls should bear this in mind, and provide skilled musicians for the evening.

Invitations to a ball or dance should be issued in the name of the lady of the house, and written on small note paper of the best quality. Elegant printed forms, some of them printed in gold or silver, are to be had at every stationer's by those who prefer them. The paper may be gilt edged, but not colored.

An invitation to a ball should be sent out at least ten days before the evening appointed. A fortnight, and even a month, may be allowed in the way of notice.

Not more than two or three days should be permitted to elapse before you reply to an invitation of this kind. The reply should always be addressed to the lady of the house.

The old style of "presenting compliments" in invitations is now absolute among cultured society people, and the proper form now is to "request the honor" of the invited, to which the latter should respond that they "have much pleasure" in accepting. If unable to accept, regrets should immediately be forwarded.

The lady who gives a ball, (we use the word to signify a private party where there is dancing, as well as a public ball), should endeavor to secure an equal number of dancers of both sexes. Many private parties are spoiled by the preponderance of young ladies, some of whom never get partners at all, unless they dance with each other.

A room should in all cases be provided for the accommodation of the ladies. In this room there ought to be several looking glasses; attendants to assist the fair visitors in the arrangement of their hair and dress; and some place in which the cloaks and wraps can be laid in order, and found at a moment's notice. Needles and thread should also be at hand, to repair any little accident incurred in dancing.

Another room should be devoted to refreshments, and kept amply supplied with coffee, lemonade, ices, wines and biscuits during the evening.

The question of supper entirely depends upon the means of those who give a ball or evening party. Where the cost is not taken into account, it is preferable to have a whole supper, with all the appliances, furnished by some outside caterer. This plan saves much trouble to the entertainers or their servants, and relieves the hostess of every anxiety. Where such a course would be imprudent, by reason of many circumstances, we would observe that a home provided supper, however simple, should be good of its kind, and abundant in quantity. Dancers are generally hungry people, and feel much aggrieved if the supply proves unequal to the demand.

On entering the ball room, the visitor should at once seek the lady of the house and pay his respects to her. He may then exchange salutations with such friends and acquaintances as may be in the room.

If the ball be a public one, and a gentleman desires to dance with any lady to whom he is a stranger, he must apply to a member of the floor committee for an introduction. Even in private balls no gentleman can invite a lady to dance without a previous introduction; and this should be effected through the lady of the house or a member of her family.

No lady should accept an invitation to dance from a gentleman to whom she has not been introduced. In case any gentleman should commit the error of so inviting her, she should not excuse herself on the plea of another or previous engagement, or of fatigue, as to do so would imply that she did not herself attach due importance to the necessary ceremony of introduction. Her best reply would be to the effect that she would have much pleasure in accepting his invitation if he would procure an introduction to her. This observation applies only to public balls. At a private party the host and hostess are sufficient guarantees for the respectability of their guests; and although a gentleman would show a singular want of knowledge of the laws of society in acting as we have supposed, the lady who should reply to him as if he were merely an impertinent stranger in a public assembly room would be implying an affront to her entertainers. The mere fact of being assembled together under the roof of a mutual friend, is in itself a kind of general introduction of the guests to each other.

An introduction given for the mere purpose of enabling a lady and gentleman to go through a dance together does not constitute an acquaintanceship. The lady is at liberty, should she feel like doing so, to pass the gentleman the next day without recognition.

To attempt to dance without a knowledge of dancing is not only to make one's self ridiculous, but one's partner also. No lady or gentleman has a right to place a partner in this absurd position.

It is not necessary that a lady or gentleman should be acquainted with the steps in order to walk gracefully and easily through a quadrille. An easy carriage and a knowledge of the figure is all that is requisite. A round dance, however, should on no account be attempted without a thorough knowledge of the steps and some previous practice.

No person who has not a good ear for time and tune need hope to dance well.

At the conclusion of a dance the gentleman bows to his partner, and either promenades with her round the room or takes her to a seat. Where a room is set apart for refreshments he offers to conduct her thither. At a public ball no gentleman would, of course, permit a lady to pay for refreshments.

Good taste forbids that a lady and gentleman should dance too frequently together at either a public or private ball. Engaged persons should be careful not to commit this conspicuous solecism.

If a lady happens to forget a previous engagement, and stands up with another partner, the gentleman whom she has thus slighted is bound to believe that she has acted from mere inadvertence, and should by no means suffer his pride to master his good temper. To cause a disagreeable scene in a private ball room is to affront your host and hostess, and to make yourself absurd. In a public room it is no less reprehensible.

Gentlemen who dance cannot be too careful not to injure the dresses of the ladies who do them the honor to stand up with them. There are some who are singularly careless in this respect, and seem to think the mischief they have done scarce worth an apology.

A gentleman conducts his last partner to the supper room, and having waited upon her while there, re-conducts her to the ball-room.

Never attempt to take a place in a dance which has been previously engaged.

A thoughtful hostess will never introduce a bad dancer to a good one, because she has no right to punish one friend in order to oblige another.

It is not customary for married persons to dance together in society.

A lady who declines dancing on the pretext of fatigue must dance no more, unless she has said she wished to rest for that dance alone.

If a lady decline dancing with a gentleman, it is rude for him to turn from her to another lady who has heard the refusal, and invite her to dance. If the first lady has a prior engagement, he must seek another partner in another part of the room ; if she refuses from fatigue or a disinclination to dance that set, it is a compliment to her for him to remain beside her, and endeavor to entertain her while the dance is in progress.

A lady should never give her bouquet, gloves, and fan to a gentleman to hold during a dance, unless he is her husband, brother or escort for the evening.

A gentleman, in waltzing with a young lady, must never encircle her waist until the dance actually commences, and drop his arm from around her as soon as the music ceases. He should perfectly understand the most delicate way of dancing this, to many, objectionable dance, and above all, how to hold a lady lightly and firmly without embracing her.

When a lady expresses a desire to sit down before the close of a dance, it is exceedingly rude for a gentleman to insist upon a continuation of the dance. He must escort her to a seat at once, and then express his regret at the interrupted pleasure. She may with propriety release him to seek another partner, but it is a poor compliment for him to accept the proposal.

A lady must be very careful not to engage herself to two gentlemen for the same dance, unless, for a round dance, she states : "I am engaged for the first half of the waltz, but will dance the second part with you." In that case, she must tell her first partner of her second engagement, that she may not offend him when she takes another partner after leaving him.

If a lady wishes to decline dancing, whether from dislike to the gentleman who invites her, or from whatever cause, she must make some excuse; but she must never refuse point blank, nor must she, after having refused to dance with one gentleman, consent to dance with another.

Every gentleman must make a point of inviting the ladies of the house to dance; and if he be kind, he will certainly devote himself— for a portion of the evening, at least—to those ladies for whom the May of life has bloomed and passed away, and who generally sit round the room looking wistfully disconsolate.

No gentleman should linger round the supper table or room. Your hostess invites you to a ball to dance, and be agreeable, not to haunt her supper room, as if you were starving.

When you have taken your position in a set, never leave it to join another, either to be among friends or to secure a better place. This is a great breach of etiquette and productive of great offence to the set which you have left. However, should any dispute arise regarding the place, never parley about the matter, but quietly and courteously resign it to the party claiming it, then it is admissable to seek another set.

A ball-room is a place of enjoyment and pleasure, not a stage for the exhibition of fancy dancing. This should be kept in mind by those who indulge during the square dances in exaggerated and grotesque movements, in order to display their suppleness or superiority in the art of dancing. Dance quietly and in accordance with the music, never endeavoring to attract attention to or remarks upon your execution.

Withdraw from a ball-room as quietly as possible, so that your departure be unobserved and consequently no signal for the entertainment to break up.

Traveling.

As a general rule, travelers are selfish. They pay little attention either to the comforts or distresses of their fellow-travelers; and the commonest observances of politeness are often sadly neglected by them. In the scramble for tickets, for seats, for state-rooms, or for places at a public table, the courtesies of life seem to be trampled under foot. Even the ladies are sometimes rudely treated and shamefully neglected in the headlong rush for desirable seats in the railway cars. To see the behavior of American people on their travels, one would suppose that we were anything but a refined nation; and I have often wondered whether a majority of our travelers could really make a decent appearance in social society.

When you are traveling, it is no excuse that because others outrage decency and propriety you should follow their example, and fight them with their own weapons. A rush and scramble at the railway ticket office is always unnecessary. The cars will not leave until every passenger is aboard, and if you have ladies with you, you can easily secure your seats and afterward procure the tickets at leisure. But suppose you do lose a favorite seat by your moderation! Is it not better to suffer a little inconvenience than to show yourself decidedly vulgar? Go to the cars half an hour before they start, and you will avoid all trouble of this kind.

When seated, or about to seat yourself in the cars, never allow considerations of personal comfort or convenience to cause you to disregard the rights of fellow-travelers, or forget the respectful courtesy due to woman. The pleasantest or most comfortable seats belong to the ladies, and you should never refuse to resign such seats to them with a cheerful politeness. Sometimes a gentleman will go through a car and choose his seat, and afterwards vacate it to procure his ticket, leaving his overcoat or carpet bag to show that the seat is taken. Always respect this token, and never seize upon a seat thus secured, without leave, even though you may want it for a lady. It is not always necessary for a gentleman to rise after he has seated himself and offer his seat to a lady, particularly if the lady is accompanied by another gentleman; for there may still be eligible vacant seats in the cars. But should you see a lady come alone, and if the seats in the car all appear to be filled, do not hesitate to offer her yours, if you have no ladies in your company. And should a lady motion to seat herself beside you, rise at once and offer her the choice of the two seats. These are but common courtesies that every well-bred man will at all times cheerfully offer to the other sex.

Making acquaintances in the cars, although correct enough, is a measure of which travelers generally appear to be very shy. There is no reason for this, as acquaintances thus picked up need never be recognized again unless you please. If a stranger speaks to you, always answer him politely, and if his conversation proves disagreeable, you have no alternative but to change your seat.

In steamers do not make a rush for the supper table, or make a glutton of yourself when you get there. Never fail to offer your seat on deck to a lady, if the seats all appear to be occupied, and always meet half way any fellow-passenger who wishes to enter into conversation with you. Some travelers are so exclusive that they consider it a presumption on the part of a stranger to address them; but such people are generally foolish, and of no account. Sociable intercourse while traveling is one of its main attractions. Who would care about sitting and moping for a dozen hours on board a steamer without exchanging a word with anybody? and this must be the fate of the exclusives when they travel alone. Even ladies, who run greater risks in forming steamboat acquaintances than the men, are allowed the greatest privileges in that respect. It might not be exactly correct for a lady to make a speaking acquaintance of a gentleman; but she may address or question him for the time being without impropriety.

Fellow-passengers, whether on a steamboat or in the cars, should at all times be sociable and obliging to one another. Those who are the reverse of this may be set down either as selfish, foolish or conceited.

In the cars you have no right to keep a window open for your accommodation, if the current of air thus produced annoys or endangers the health of another. There are a sufficient number of discomforts in traveling, at best, and it should be the aim of each passenger to lessen them as much as possible, and to cheerfully bear his own part. Life is a journey, and we are all fellow-travelers.

If in riding in an omnibus, or crossing a ferry with a friend, he wishes to pay for you, never insist upon paying for yourself or for both. If he is before you, let the matter pass without remark.

When traveling, a gentleman may say as many civil and complimentary things to a lady as can be introduced, in an easy, graceful and unconstrained manner, free from all appearance of low gallantry: it casts an air of friendly feeling around you. Listen to their prosing, but never expose their ignorance, when you detect it: it vexes them, and does you no good. Look at the people, the sights, scenery and monuments with your own eyes; form your own opinions, aided by the best information you can obtain; and do not follow servilely the track of the would-be liberal tourists of the modern school, who admire every thing in proportion as it deviates from what is foreign. If you have traveled in a frank and cheerful mood, then it will be delightful to discuss your adventures with the intelligent and instructed; again to laugh at what was ridiculous, and grieve over scenes that awakened thoughts of sorrow. It will be profitable also to compare notes with the judicious and observing, and try the value of your own opinions, by those which others may have formed on similar subjects.

Traveling may prove agreeable and beneficial; but it may become injurious also. Persons of talents and education, who have traveled much, have invariably returned to their native land confirmed in patriotism, and grateful also for the many advantages possessed by this country over all the other nations of the world. The secondary class, on the contrary—and they are of course the most numerous—think it necessary, in order to be looked upon as persons of taste, to discover something vastly fine in everything that is foreign; and always return in perfect rapture with continental cooking, dancing, fiddling and singing; extolling the languages, literature and manners of foreign countries far above those of their native land.

Some of these, after a foreign trip, even ape the manners and customs of the countries they have visited, and would fain establish them in their native land, to the overthrow of all rules, laws and general government firmly established long before some of them emerged fiom their swaddling clothes. They do not, because they will not, realize that they provoke the contempt of the truly wise, great and good, and that their animadversions are received with scoffs and sneers from even the illiterate and lowly minded. Truly it may be said that society is no better for *their* being in it.

Amusements.

A gentleman who wishes to invite a young lady, who is not related to him, to visit any place of public amusement with him, must, the first time that he invites her, also invite another lady of the same family to accompany her. No young lady should visit public places of amusement with a gentleman with whom she is but slightly acquainted, alone.

It is a gentleman's duty to invite a lady long enough before the evening of the performance to be certain of securing pleasant seats, as it is but a poor compliment to take her where she will be uncomfortable, or where she can neither hear nor see.

Although a carriage may not be necessary on account of the weather, it is a more elegant way of paying attention to a lady to provide one.

Never assume an air of secrecy or mystery in a public place; and even if you have the right to do so, assume no lover-like airs. It is rude to converse loudly, especially during the performance; but a low tone is all that is necessary, not a whisper.

To appear to comment aside upon those near you is extremely ill-bred.

A lady is not expected to bow to a friend across a theatre or concert-room; but a gentleman may recognize his lady friends.

A lady must answer a note of invitation to visit a place of public amusement as soon as possible, as, by delay, she may keep her gentleman friend in doubt, and deprive him of the pleasure of inviting another friend if she declines.

It is ill-bred to arrive late at any public entertainment, and looks as if you were not sufficiently master of your own time to be punctual.

In a theatre, give your attention entirely to the stage when the curtain is up; to your companion when it is down.

It looks badly to see a lady staring round the house with an opera glass. Never is a modest dignity more becoming than in a theatre. To indulge in extravagant gesture, laugh boisterously, flirt a fan conspicuously, toy with an eyeglass or opera glass, indulge in lounging attitudes, whisper aside, are all unlady-like in the extreme.

Boisterous applause and loud laughter are ungentlemanly.

It is in bad taste to distract your companion's interest from the performance, even if you find it dull yourself.

No gentleman should leave a lady alone for a moment in a public place of amusement. He may subject her to annoyance, or he may find another lady in his seat when he returns, which would separate him from his companion until the close of the performance; for, although a gentleman when alone should offer his seat to a lady or old gentleman who cannot procure one, he is not expected to do so when escorting a lady. His place is then that of protector to his charge, and he must not relinquish it for a moment.

Secure a libretto, or programme, before taking your seat, that you may not be obliged to rise to get one.

At the opera, conversation during the performance is in the worst taste. The lowest tone will disturb the real lovers of music. Exclamations of "Lovely!" "Exquisite!" "How sweet!" and others, are all proofs of vulgarity.

If you promenade at a concert or between the acts at a theatre, you may bow to friends the first time you pass them only. A lady must not allow other gentlemen to join her, if she would not offend her escort, and no gentleman will stop a lady to speak to her. A conversation of a moment or two is all that is allowable in such meetings.

If seats are secured, it is best to arrive about five minutes before the commencement of a performance; but if a gentleman is escorting a lady to an entertainment where seats cannot be secured, he should call for her at an early hour, that she may get a good place.

If you speak to your companion during the performance, do so in a low tone, that you may not disturb those who are near you and wish to hear the actors.

In entering a concert-room or the box of a theatre, a gentleman should precede a lady, if there is not room to walk beside her, until they reach the seats, then hand her to the inner one, taking the outside one himself. In going out, if he cannot offer her his arm, he must again walk before her, until he reaches the lobby, and then offer her his arm.

In a picture-gallery, never stand conversing before the paintings in such a way as to interrupt the view of others. If you wish to converse, stand aside or take seats and do so.

A gentleman alone may join lady friends for a few moments between the acts at a theatre, or in the intermission at a concert, but only for a few moments, as their escort has a prior claim upon their attention.

It is an act of rudeness to join any party about to visit a place of amusement, or at one, unless urgently invited, and no one of taste will ever form a third. If two or three ladies are in the party and but one gentleman, another gentleman, if well acquainted, may offer his services as escort to one of the ladies, and if not allowed to share the expenses, should invite the party to partake of refreshments after the performance is over.

Always enter a concert-hall or lecture-room as quietly as possible.

Never push violently through a crowd at a public place. A lady will always find room made for her if she requests it, or if it is requested by her escort.

After escorting a lady to a place of amusement, a gentleman may ask permission to call the following morning or evening, and the lady must be at home to receive that call. She should take that opportunity to thank him for the pleasure she has enjoyed, and find some warm words of praise for the performance. To severely criticize on such an occasion is rude to the escort, who has intended to give pleasure, and the performance must be bad indeed where nothing can be found to merit a word of praise.

In visiting a fancy fair, too many persons act as if they were in a store, cheapening the articles offered for sale, and being careless about their criticisms and remarks. It is impossible to tell who may be wounded by such conduct. The very lady who offers you an article you pronounce "absolutely hideous" may have spent hours in its manufacture, and feel proportionately hurt at your remarks. Courtesy and words of praise are never more appreciated than by those who have spent weary hours in preparing for this most troublesome of all charities.

On the other hand, the position of a lady at the table of a fancy fair is necessarily an exposed one, and requires a great amount of modest dignity to support it. Flirting, loud talking, importunate entreaties to unwilling friends to buy your goods, are all in bad taste; and it is equally bad to leave your place every few moments to visit the refreshment-table in company with your gentlemen friends. We heard a lady boast once that she had been seventeen times in one day to the refreshment-table "for the good of the fair," and we could not but think the cause might have been aided without quite such a display of gastronomic energy. No true lady will follow friends all around the room offering goods for sale, nor force articles on reluctant purchasers by appealing to their gallantry.

In entering a fancy fair where many ladies are present, strict etiquette requires a gentleman to remove his hat, and carry it whilst in the room, but it is a rule much neglected.

It is rude for a lady to take advantage of the rule which prevents a gentleman from asking for change at a fair. If he says, in presenting a larger amount than the purchased article calls for, "Pray accept the balance for the object for which you are working," she may, of course, place the gift in her cash-box; otherwise it is more lady-like to give back the change.

Servants.

Conduct towards servants should be always equal, never violent, never familiar. Speak to them always with civility, but keep them in their proper places.

Give no occasion for them to complain of you; but never suffer yourself to complain of them without first ascertaining that your complaint is just, seeing that it has attention, and that the fault complained of is remedied.

Beware of giving servants the inch; there is no class so prone under such circumstances, to take the ell.

If staying in a friend's house, you may assume, to a certain extent, that your friend's servants are your servants. But this must be only so far as you are yourself concerned. You must not, on any account, give directions respecting the general conduct of the *ménage*. For all your own personal wants, however, you are free to command their services. Ask for anything, under their control, that may be lacking in your own room; for whatever you need at meal times; let them call you in the morning if you sleep soundly; do not send them on errands, however, without first ascertaining that it will not interfere with their regular routine of household duty; but do anything and everything required for your own personal convenience and comfort through the servants. It is contrary to all laws of etiquette to trouble your host or hostess with all your petty wants.

A man-servant is rarely grateful, and seldom attached. He is generally incapable of appreciating those advantages which, with your cultivated judgment, you know to be most conducive to his welfare. Do you accord to him regular hours, and a stated allowance of work; do you refrain from sending him out because it is wet, and he is unwell; do you serve yourself rather than ring for him at dinner time, he will rarely have the grace to thank you in his heart for your constant consideration.

Servants' sympathies are with their equals. They feel for a poor servant run off his legs, and moped to death; they have no feeling for a painstaking mistress, economical both from principle and scanty means; they would (most of them) see her property wasted, and her confidence abused without compunction. It is the last effort of virtue in a servant, if, without any private reason, he should discharge his duty by informing you of the injury which you are enduring at the hands of his fellow servant. It is an effort of virtue, for it will bring down many a bitter taunt and hard word upon his faithful head.

There is one thing a man servant values beyond all that your kindness and consideration can do for him—his liberty; liberty to eat, drink and be merry, with your things, in the company of his own friends; and the housemaid wishes for liberty to lie in bed in the morning, because she was up late the previous night. The cook desires liberty, also. For this liberty, if you grant it, they will despise you; if you deny it, they will respect you. Aim at their esteem; despair of their love or gratitude; make your place what the best class of servants will value, and though in their heart they may not thank you for it, you will gain, perhaps, one servant out of twenty who will keep gross imposition and gross immorality at bay.

These remarks are not intended to deny the warm attachment of female servants to the children of their employers. Deep love, no doubt, is lavished by many a woman on the babe she has nursed. There is a great deal to be said on the chapter of nurses, which would require to be dealt with by itself. Much wisdom is required in the administration of a nursery, to which but few general rules would apply. Cruel is the tyranny the nurse frequently practises on the parent, who often refrains from entering her nursery, not from want of love for her children, but positive dread of the sour looks which greet her. Let her be firm; let no shrinking from grieving her darling, who would 'break his heart if his Nana went,' deter her from discharging the encroaching servant.

On the choice of servants much of the comfort of the young house-keeper depends. It often happens that her choice has been determined by appearance rather than the value of character. If such be the case, she will have many difficulties to encounter. It is, in the present day, hardly safe to take a servant if there be a single objection to character, however it may be glossed over by the person referred to on this point; for there is now an unhealthy disposition to pass over the failings of servants who have left their places, and to make them perfect in the eyes of others. In respect to sobriety, many people will not acknowledge that a servant had had the vice of drinking, but will cover the unpleasant truth with such gentle and plausible terms that it becomes difficult to comprehend how far the hint is grounded, or not. Be assured when a lady or gentleman hesitates on this point, or on that of honesty, it is wiser not to engage a servant. Nor are you deviating from Christian charity in not overlooking a dereliction of so material a sort. The kindest plan to the vast community of domestic servants is to be rigid in all important points, and, having, after a due experience, a just confidence in them, to be somewhat more indulgent to errors of a more trivial nature.

Be very careful not to let your servant suppose you cannot part with her. Treat her with confidence, but with strict impartiality; reprove where necessary, mildly, but decidedly, lest she should presume, and compel you, if you would retain your freedom, to let her go.

Over-indulgence towards servants is to be deprecated. Formerly they were treated with real kindness, but it was the kindness that exacted duty in return, and took a real interest in the welfare of each servant. The reciprocal tie in former times between servant and master was strong; now it is wholly gone. The easy rule of masters and mistresses proceeds far more from indifference than from kindness of heart; for the real charity is to keep servants steadily to their duties. They are a class of persons to whom much leisure is destruction; the pursuits of their idle hours are seldom advantageous to them, and theirs are not minds, generally, which can thrive in repose. Idleness, to them, is peculiarly the root of all evil; for if their time is not spent in vicious amusements, it is often passed in scandal, discontent, and vanity. In writing thus, I do not recommend a hard or inconsiderate system to servants. They require, and in many instances they merit, all that can be done to alleviate a situation of servitude. They ought not to be the slaves of caprice or the victims of temper. Their work should be measured out with a just hand; but it should be regularly exacted in as much perfection as can be expected in variable and erring human nature.

Another point which demands firmness is that of early hours. In this respect, example is as important as precept; but, however uncertain you may be yourself, do not relax a rule of this kind; for every comfort during the day depends on the early rising of your servants. Without this, all their several departments are hurried through or neglected in some important respect.

Your mode of address to servants must be decisive, yet mild. The authoritative tone is not to be recommended. It is very unbecoming to any young person, and it rarely attains the end desired; but there is a quiet dignity of deportment which few servants ever can resist. This should be tempered with kindness, when circumstances call it forth, but should never descend to familiarity; for no caution is more truly kind than that which confines servants strictly to their own sphere.

Much evil results from the tendency, more especially of the very young or of very old mistresses of families, to partiality. Commonly, one servant becomes the almost avowed favorite; and it is difficult to say whether that display of partiality is the more pernicious to the servant who is the object of it, or to the rankling and jealous minds of the rest of the household. It is true that it is quite impossible to avoid entertaining a greater degree of confidence in some servants than in others; but it should be shown with a due regard to the feelings of all. It is, of course, allowable towards those who take a decidedly responsible and confidential situation in a household. Still, never let such persons assume the reins of government; let them act the part of helmsmen to the vessel, but not aspire to the control of the captain.

It is generally wise and right, after a due experience of the principles and intentions of servants, to place confidence in their honesty, and to let them have the comfort of knowing that you do so. At the same time, never cease to exercise a system of supervision. The great principle of housekeeping is regularity, and without this (one of the most difficult of the minor virtues to practise), all efforts to promote order must be ineffectual. There are energetic women, clever and well-intentioned, who fail in attaining a good method, owing to their being uncertain in hours, governed by impulse, and capricious. And there are, also, women, inferior in capacity, slow, and apathetic, who make excellent heads of families, as far as their household was concerned, from their steadiness and regularity. Their very power of enduring monotony has been favorable to their success in this way, especially if they are not called upon to act in peculiar and difficult cases, in which their actual inferiority is traceable. But these are not the ordinary circumstances of life.

In this country, servants are proverbially more troublesome than in

Europe, where service is often transmitted through generations in one family. Here, the housekeeper is obliged to change often, taking frequently the most ignorant of the lower classes of foreigners to train into good and useful servants, only to have them become dissatisfied as soon as they become acquainted with others, who instil the republican doctrine of perfect equality into their minds, ruining them for good servants. There are some points of etiquette, however, upon which every lady should insist:

Never allow a servant to keep people waiting upon the doorstep.

Never allow servants to treat any one disrespectfully.

Never allow servants to turn their own proper duties over to the children or other servants by a bribe. Many fond parents would be amazed if they knew how much running and actual work was performed by their children, and how many fits of mysterious indigestion were caused by the rich cake, candy, or half ripe fruit that paid for the service and bribed the silence.

Never allow a servant to keep a visitor standing parleying on the doorstep, while she holds the door ajar. Train the door servant to admit any caller promptly, show them to the parlor, bring up their cards at once, and return with your answer or message.

Hotel Etiquette.

When a lady arrives alone at a hotel, she should, if possible, be provided with a letter of introduction to the proprietor; she should send for him immediately upon her arrival, present her letter, or her card, and mention the time for which she desires to secure a room.

In going to meals, a lady should request one of the waiters to meet her at the dining-room door, and escort her to the table, saving her the awkwardness of crossing the room alone, and showing others that she is a regular resident in the house. She may keep the services of this waiter at table during her stay, and should give him a present of money before leaving.

In giving an order at a public table, a lady should decide quickly what dishes she desires, and order them in a low but distinct tone.

No lady will stare round the room, fidget with her napkin, plate, knife or fork, play with the salt, or exhibit any awkward embarrassment, while waiting for a meal to be served. It is allowable to look over a newspaper in the interval at breakfast; but the habit, quite common, of carrying a novel to the table is not ladylike.

If a lady accepts any civility from a gentleman at the same table, such as placing butter, sugar, or water nearer to her plate, she must thank him; but by no means start a conversation with him.

If a lady have friends at the table, she may converse in a low, quiet tone; but any loud tone, laughing extravagantly, or gesticulations, are exceedingly ill-bred. To comment upon others present, either aloud or in a whisper, is extremely rude.

A lady must never point to any dish she wishes passed to her. If she cannot call it by name, a welltrained waiter will know her wishes if she looks at the dish.

Any bold action or boisterous deportment in a hotel will expose a lady to the most severe censure of the refined around her, and may render her liable to misconstruction, and impertinence.

Greetings offered by other ladies at the table, or in the parlor, should not be too hastily checked, as the acquaintance so formed is never required by etiquette to be recognized elsewhere.

A lady alone at a hotel should wear the most modest and least conspicuous dress appropriate to the hour of the day. Full dress must not be worn unless she has an escort present.

A lady should never go alone to the supper table after ten o'clock. If she returns from an entertainment at a later hour, and has no escort to supper, she should have that meal sent to her room.

A lady should carefully lock her trunks before leaving her room at a hotel, and should give her purse and jewelry into the care of the proprietor on her arrival, ringing for them if she requires them during her stay.

No lady should open a window in a hotel parlor, if there are other ladies near it, without first ascertaining that it will not inconvenience them.

No lady should use the piano of a hotel uninvited if there are others in the room. It looks bold and forward to display even the most finished musical education in this way. It is still worse to sing.

A lady should never go herself to the door of a hotel to call a hack. Ring for a servant to perform this office, and he will bring the hack to the ladies' entrance.

No lady should stand or linger in the halls of a hotel, but pass through them quietly never stopping alone for a moment.

No lady should stand alone at the front windows of a hotel parlor, nor may she walk out on the porch, or, indeed, any conspicuous place.

A lady is not expected to recognize her friends across the parlor or dining-room of a hotel.

No scolding of servants is permissible in a hotel. If they are negligent or disrespectful, complain to the housekeeper or landlord; it is their business to keep the domestics in order, not that of their guests.

For a lady to go up the stairs of a hotel singing is ill-bred, and may expose her to rudeness.

It is a breach of etiquette to take any newspaper, book, or music you may find in a hotel parlor to your own room, even if you return it.

Lolling or lounging in a public parlor can never be permitted to a lady.

It is a breach of etiquette for a lady to touch her baggage in a hotel after it is packed. There are plenty of servants to attend to it, and they should carry to the hack even the travelling-shawl, satchel, and railway novel. Nothing looks more awkward than to see a lady, with both hands full, stumbling up the steps of a hotel hack.

No lady must ever pass in or out at the public entrance of a hotel. There is always an entrance for ladies especially, and it is bold and unbecoming for them to be seen in the one appropriated to gentlemen.

A gentleman who will escort a lady through the public entrance shows a lamentable ignorance of the usages of hotel life.

Mourning.

During times of health and happiness it is perhaps rather trying to be asked to turn our thoughts into doleful channels; but sooner or later the sad time comes, for "Who breathes must suffer and who thinks must mourn," and we have to turn our minds to the inevitable and share the common lot of man. In times of mourning it seems doubly hard to arouse ourselves and allow the question of what to wear to intrude itself. Custom decrees, if even inclination does not prompt us, to show in some outward degree our respect for the dead by wearing the usual black.

We do not advise people to rush into black for every slight bereavement, nor, on the other hand, to show the utter disregard some do on the death of their relations, and only acknowledge the departure of those near and dear to them by a band of crape round the arm. This is the mark of mourning adopted by those in the services who have to wear uniform, but not a fitting way of outwardly showing respect to the memory of those who have been called away from us and whose loss we deplore. We once noted the appearance of a lady in a new ruby satin dress, with a band of crape around her arm. The fact of the dress being new, showed that poverty did not cause this incongruity. It is hardly ever those who are styled "the poor" who so err against the accepted ideas of decency and respect. They always, however straitened they may be in circumstances, contrive to wear mourning for their deceased relatives. When black is fashionable, no difficulty is found in wearing it, and you meet all your friends so attired, but when it becomes a question of duty, then objections are raised as to the unnecessary expense and the inconvenience of so dressing. The majority adhere in this respect to the customs their parents have followed; but the advanced few are those who air such sentiments, talk of the "mourning of the heart, not mere outward woe," and, not wearing what is really mourning, go into society on the plea, "Oh! we know that those who are gone would not wish us to grieve for them." This may be all very well, but in the case of husbands, wives, parents, brothers, sisters, aunts, uncles, and the nearer related cousins, decency requires some outward mark of respect to their memory.

The first mourning is worn for twelve months. Second mourning twelve months also; the cap in second mourning is left off. Elderly widows frequently remain in mourning for long periods, if not for the remainder of their lives, retaining the widow's cap, collar and cuffs, but leaving off the deep crape the second year, and afterwards entirely discarding crape.

The mourning for parents ranks next to that of widows; for children by their parents, and for parents by their children, these being of course identical in degree.   It lasts in either case twelve months, six months in crape trimmings, three in plain black, and three in half mourning.   It is, however, better taste to continue the plain black to the end of the year, and wear half mourning for three months longer.

Many persons think it is in better taste not to commence half mourning until after the expiration of a year, except in the case of young children, who are rarely kept in mourning beyond the twelve months.

A wife should wear just the same mourning for her husband's relations as for her own; thus, if her husband's mother died, she would wear mourning as deep as if for her own mother.

No invitations would be accepted before the funeral of any relatives closely enough related to you to put on mourning for.   In the case of brothers, sisters, parents and grand parents, society would be given up for at least three months, if not more, and it would be very bad taste to go to a ball or large festive gathering in crape.   Widows do not enter society for at least a year, that is, during the period of their deepest mourning.   With regard to *complimentary* mourning as worn by mothers for the mother or father-in-law of their married children, black would be worn for six weeks or so without crape; by second wives for the parents of the first wife, for about three weeks, and in a few other cases.

It is better taste to wear mourning in making the first call after a bereavement on friends, but this is not a decided rule, only a graceful method of implying sympathy with those who are suffering affliction. But calls are not made until the cards with "thanks for kind inquiries" have been sent in return for the cards left at the time of decease. Letters of condolence should always be written on slightly black edged paper, and it would be kind to intimate in the letter that no answer to it will be expected.   Few realize the effort it is to those left to sit down and write answers to inquiries and letters, however kind and sympathizing they may have been.

Servants are not usually put into mourning except for the members of the household in which they are living, not for the relations of their masters and mistresses, and very frequently only for the heads of the house, not for the junior members.

Mourning has generally to be purchased hurriedly, and too often a dress-maker gets *carte blanche* almost to furnish the mourning. When such is the case, no wonder mourning is considered expensive; for things which are quite unnecessary, such as expensive crape in the place of rain-proof kinds, more crape used than the degree of mourning requires, and many extravagancies of a like nature, naturally swell such a bill into one of large proportions, when by a little forethought the necessary black could have been purchased at a far more reasonable rate.

It is not necessary to have very expensive mourning if our means will not allow it; we must suit our requirement to the state of our purses. But we sincerely trust the old custom of wearing decent mourning for those taken away from us will never be really discontinued in America, for it is one of those proofs of our home affections which can never be done away with without a loss of national respect.

Funerals.

The consignment of "dust to dust" is the saddest of all the ceremonies of this life, calling forth the sympathy alike of friends and relatives, and a delicate consideration for the bereaved ones and fitting respect for the melancholy occasion should be evinced.

In entering the house of mourning, a gentleman must remove his hat in the hall, and not replace it while in the house.

Loud talking in the chamber of death is a rudeness which shows not only a want of respect for the dead, but a want of consideration for the grief of the survivors.

All quarrels must be forgotten in the presence of death. Enemies who meet at a funeral are bound by etiquette, if not by feeling, to salute each other with quiet gravity.

Whilst the body of the dead remains in the house, no visitor must expect to see the members of the bereaved family, and no offence may be taken if admission is refused to the nearest friends.

The formalities necessary upon the death of a member of a family entail upon the survivors many painful interviews, many directions, and often most harrowing discussions. It is, therefore, customary to entrust these details to some relative or friend, who, while near enough to carefully direct the affairs, is yet able to bear the trying details better than the members of the immediate family. It is best to select some one accustomed to the discharge of this duty, and more prudent to name a limit for the expenses.

Where there are no funeral arrangements made in the will, the person taking this charge may ask one interview with the nearest relative, but after that, relieve them of all care in the matter. If there is no friend who can undertake these trying duties, it is then customary to make the undertaker the master of the painful ceremonies.

To surround the funeral ceremonies with great parade and pomp is usually more of a vain and ostentatious display than an act of respect towards the dead; at the same time, any meanness or parsimony is in bad taste. The expenses should be governed by the position of the deceased, and the means of the survivors.

A list of the persons invited must be given to the person directing the funeral ceremonies, and he will give the under'aker a list of the order in which the guests are to be placed in the carriages, if the place of sepulture is some distance from where the ceremonies are held, or the order of the procession if the guests go thereto on foot.

Guests should not present themselves at a funeral before the hour appointed, the family paying their last sad visit to the coffin previous to that hour, when all intrusion upon them is a breach of good manners.

The remains are usually exposed in the parlor, while the family congregate in another room. As the period approaches for the last visit, the undertaker will notify the family, who, after paying the last respects to the remains, will immediately return to the apartment from which they issued, remaining there until the close of the ceremony.

In case of the services being held in church, the remains are placed in front of the chancel, the lid removed, and the friends (at the end of the service) will pass from the feet to the head, up one aisle and down another.

Should the funeral take place at the house, it is proper that some relative not immediately connected with the family of the deceased should receive the guests and do the honors of the occasion.

Strict etiquette denies the ladies of the house the privilege of following the remains to the grave; but it is a custom "more honored on the breach than the observance."

When the funeral procession is ready to start, the clergyman leaves the house first, and enters a carriage, which precedes the hearse. Then follows the coffin, which is placed in the hearse; the next carriage is for the immediate family and relatives. Guests stand uncovered while these mourners pass them, no salutation being expected.

The gentleman who does the honors should precede the family as they pass from their room to the carriages, assist them in, close the door, and motion the driver to move slowly forward, and to the next carriage to drive up to the door.

The same order is observed at the church door, where the master of ceremonies assists the mourners to leave and re-enter the carriages.

When the private carriage of the deceased follows the hearse, it should be empty, and precede the other carriages.

If the friends go on foot, and the weather is cold, the gentlemen may wear their hats; but if the weather is mild, it is customary to walk uncovered, with the hat in the right hand.

If the hat is worn, it must be removed as the coffin passes from the hearse to the church, when the guests form a double line, down which it is carried, and the same line and observance must be made after the service, as the coffin is carried from the church to the hearse again.

If lady friends attend a funeral, if they are not in mourning, they should wear grave, quite colors. To go to a funeral in a gay dress is insulting.

Upon the coffin of an infant or young person, it is customary to place a wreath of white flowers.

Upon the coffin of a married person, a cross of white flowers is usually placed.

Upon the coffin of an army or navy officer, the hat, epaulets, sword, and sash are placed, and it is customary to use the flag to cover the coffin.

When arrived at the cemetery the clergyman walks in advance of the coffin, and the others alight from the carriages and stand around the grave.

After the carriages leave the cemetery it is not customary for the guests to return to the house of the mourners, but each may direct the driver, in a low tone, where to drive them.

The carriage must be sent for the clergyman in time for him to be punctually at the house at the appointed hour.

If gifts of flowers are sent, they must be white only, and sent on the day of the funeral early enough to be used in the decoration of the coffin.

Should pall-bearers be arranged for, they must be the nearest friends of the deceased.

If gloves and crape bands are distributed to the gentleman guests, they must be handed them when they first enter the house. It is a gross violation of etiquette to make any selection in such cases, nobody expects to have gloves so given as to fit the hands, but they must be worn. It is far preferable to present yourself with black kid gloves on your hands.

Friends in deep mourning are not expected to pay visits of condolence, and are excused from accepting funeral invitations; but all others are expected to accept them. It is but a poor compliment to your friends to attend their receptions, dinners, balls and parties and neglect to be present when they are in affliction, or to pay the last act of respect to the memory of those they love.

During the week following a funeral, friends should leave their cards for the family of the deceased, and call again about a fortnight later, asking them to see the members of the family.

It is not customary to ask to see the family of a deceased friend before the funeral; but cards should be sent and offers of service sent by note.

No member of the immediate family of the deceased should leave the house between the death and the funeral upon any errand or pretext.

At the funeral of a mounted officer, his horse, fully equipped, and draped in mourning, should be led by a servant after the hearse.

If the deceased belonged to any society, as Free Masons, Odd Fellows, or such organization, the society should be invited through a note sent to the president or chief officer, and they will send word to the master of ceremonies if there is any especial order in which they wish to follow the corpse, or any form or ceremony peculiar to that Order which they would like observed. These invitations, if given through the newspapers, should carefully specify the Lodge or Order to which the deceased belonged. The regalia in such cases is usually displayed on the coffin lid, but removed before the coffin leaves the house.

White plumes are customary on the hearse of a young person, and black ones for married and elderly people.

It is not customary to send invitations to the funeral of a person who has died of contagious disease, and the statement of the malady in the newspapers is generally accepted by the friends as an excuse for the omission of invitations.

In visiting a cemetery, it is an act of rudeness to stand near a lot where mourners are assembled, or in any way to notice those who are decorating the graves of friends. No time can be named when the delicate attentions and observances of etiquette are more grateful than when sorrow is heavy on the heart.

Valuable Accomplishments,

AND WHAT TO AVOID IF YOU WOULD SECURE A DESIRABLE POSITION IN SOCIETY.

There are many fields from which to choose accomplishments—science, literature, the arts, and others, according to the taste of the chooser.

Science, or the knowledge of things, is as wide as creation, and as interesting to intelligent minds. Its wonders are inexhaustible; and he who is conversant with them can always have it in his power to promote conversation of the loftiest kind. He is the privileged exhibitor of the beautiful spectacle of the universe, and his intelligent audience gladly pay him for his entertainment, by feelings of gratitude, admiration, and respect.

Literature is one in which elegant minds delight to shine. In this, human nature refines itself by finding itself mirrored back in ideal forms. The idealization of our being need not spend itself in mere ideas. The thoughts in or minds, the words upon our lips may be purified and refined by this idealizing process couched in the study of literature, and yet be as true, as good, and as strong as before. The action too is not impaired—it is that of a higher being.

Both science and literature have great thoughts for expression, and he who can express them greatly will always be deemed a great man

Nor can we cultivate them without getting into the society of great men, and unconsciously borrowing something of their greatness. It is said, with a deal of truth, that a man is known by the society he keeps. If, then, you show that you have been in company of such as Homer, Shakespeare, Galileo, or Buffon, you will be known only for what is noble and good. On a woodland excursion he who can find "sermons in stones, books in the running brooks, and good in everything" will appear to greater advantage than he who babbles talk foreign to the lovely world that surrounds him, and that is constantly projecting beautiful pictures on the tablet of his mind.

A knowledge of languages, ancient or modern, or both, while their literatures, has great weight in society, and enables a man to appear more brilliant than the little "art," which shows off accomplishments that are merely surface deep. Nothing is considered more the mark of a gentleman than an acquaintance with the classics, ancient or modern.

True, it sometimes degenerates into pedantry; but that is the abuse, not the use of it. Thought is of course a higher sphere of conversation than mere language, but the Attic salt is considered best as a seasoner by average minds, and you cannot always have the pleasing of your own judgment as to what is best.

Art is another very extensive field for the display of your ability to make a shining mark. If you have the power itself it gives you more authority to speak, for you are thereby enabled to form juster opinions that can stand criticism.

But whatever range of studies you enter upon for the proper fitting out of your mind, avoid furnishing it with such articles as, however useful in their own proper sphere, are quite out of place as items of furniture in your mind.

Be very careful to eschew pedantry. A pedant is a puzzle of a man— his knowledge and his ignorance are both in extremes. He knows a huge mass of what nobody else cares to know, and does not care to know a huge mass of what everybody else would feel ashamed to be ignorant. He knows a good deal more about the Greeks and Romans than about the people he is living among. He may not be able to find his way to the next street, yet he is intimately acquainted with the buildings of ancient Rome, and the several quarters of ancient Jerusalem. He knows exactly the dimensions of the Forum Boarium, but would feel insulted by a question about those of our own bazaar. He would express extreme indignation and contempt if asked to handle a cricket bat or an oar, but he will discourse learnedly on the Trochus or the Trireme. He is not able to distinguish a quadrille from a polka, but he can detail all the evolutions of the Pyrrhic dance. He has written a dissertation on the Lydian and Dorian Moods, but he can't see any great difference between a Highland pibroch and an oratorio of Handel or Beethoven. He is equally ignorant of sculpture and painting. He talks indeed about Phidias and Praxiteles, because he finds them mentioned in his classic authors; but he puts no value on Thorwaldsen or Turner; and even when you place him before the Elgin Marbles, he feels interested in them only in so far as they settle the meaning of some disputed passage. His physician has impressed on him the necessity of exercise, but 'tis

almost a matter of course he doesn't know how to take a walk. He
sees no beauty in the face of Nature—or if there comes across his mind
a recollection of a time when he did delight to look upon it, this natural
feeling soon evaporates in a musty quotation.   Parallel passages in
Greek and Latin he can cite without limit—and there are few words
whose quantity he has not some line of poetry ready to determine.   But
worth of sentiment and felicity of expression are lost on him.   Though
he prates about the sublimity of Æschylus, and the phylosophy of
Euripides, he is not terrified by Macbeth, does not speculate with
Hamlet.   His pride comes to back his ignorance, and he regards as
vulgar and mechanical all that he does not know, and everything that
he cannot do.   He looks with affected contempt on fishing and shooting,
fencing and dancing,—he doesn't swim—he doesn't play cards, chess,
or bagatelle—he went once to the theatre to see Antigone—but he has
an infinite horror of all kinds of amusements.

We have known only one of this class who had in his composition a
fine vein of natural humor; but he is sometimes not without pretension
to wit.   He even makes puns; but the analogies he discovers have
always one term at least in the dread unknown of school cram.   He
suggests the propriety of naming streets after the five Predicables—
assigning one to people of substance—another to people of quality, etc.,
and argues against the illogical procedure of landlords who insist upon
their tenants coming to a conclusion on the subject of rent before they
have granted them the premises.   Should you happen to hear him
discoursing on some favorite theme, you might think his intellectual
activity unbounded; yet in this point he is the most slothful man alive;
he thinks none, he merely remembers.   Reading is to him just an in-
temperate habit, like dram-drinking; he has accustomed himself to a
stimulus which his enfeebled mind can no longer want.   He has become
so much habituated to the authority of books, that he has forgot that
judgment has any authority.   Although he has a prodigious acquaintance
with other people's ideas—of all people in the world he has fewest of
his own.   He looks at everything as reflected in other men's minds—.
the broad daylight streaming from the thing itself blinds him.   Books
are called spectacles through which we look at the world—to him books
are blue spectacles that keep the strong light from his weak eyes, and
tint everything with their own hue.   He thinks with his books, as a
cripple walks with his crutches, and he is always behind when the
angel comes down to stir the waters.   Thoughts that live and work in
the heart of ages acquire value to him only when he gets them served
up in printer's ink and parchment, as dilettanti care little for Pharaoh's
daughter, who walked with her maidens on the banks of the Nile, but
put great value on her when salted and swaddled and boxed in a mummy
case.   He is a very child in the ways of the world.   He doesn't take
any interest in his next-door neighbor, though he may have known him
since he was a child—he takes far more interest in the genealogies of
the Cæsars or the Scipios.   He can't appreciate honest manliness in any
but Aristides or Cato.   He can pronounce an oration on the character
of Pericles, or Pompey, but cannot tell whether or not his most intimate
friend is a knave or a numskull.   He never reads the debates in Par-
liament—but sometimes looks at the column of varieties.   He reads

some novels—Valerius and the Fawn of Sertorius—and expresses his regret that Shakespeare's Roman plays have so little of the Roman spirit. When he goes to church he uses the Greek Testament and the Septuagint—and not unfrequently laments that our vernacular has failed in expressing the force of this tense or that particle. During sermon he employs himself in reconciling Griesbach and Tischendorf, or keeps a sharp lookout for slips in the minister's grammar, or fallacies in his argument.

A one-sided being stamped with any portion of the preceding feature is certain of proving a bore in any intelligent society. He can be endured only by being made a butt for pleasantries and ridicule.

But pedantry is not confined to learning alone. There is pedantry wherever there is persevering "monotalk" on any subject, simply because we know it particularly well, to the evident "boring" of the company. Such is the case of a merchant talking "shop," or a clergyman talking "church." Remember, however, that it is not the talking well and thoroughly on a subject that constitutes pedantry. It is the keeping of it up when the others desire to let it drop, or the introduction of an *outré* subject in which the others have no common interest.

Some have a habit of preaching their opinions in conversation. This is very disagreeable and unwise. Your opinions if you wish them expressed most effectively will have a much better chance of being entertained if they are suggested modestly. Some learned men, proud of their knowledge, speak only to decide, and to let you know pretty plainly by their imperious manner that their decision is not to be appealed from. Even though they should speak nothing but the truth, men are at once inclined to dissent, and even to serve them with a return in kind. The more you know, the more modest should you be, if your knowledge has done you the good it was intended. Remember Sir Isaac Newton, who compared himself with all his learning to child gathering pebbles on the sea-shore; so little did he think of what even he had gathered on this shore of time. Even where you are sure, do not press it dogmatically; represent but do not pronounce; and if you would convince others, be open to conviction yourself.

Our modern education is becoming less and less pedantic. The ancients are not worshipped with the reverence they once were. "We are the ancients," is the common-sense cry now, for we are older in knowledge and art than they. Formerly, when Latin and Greek were the only humanities studied at the school and college, the ancients were talked of as something more than men, and the moderns as something less. Speak of the moderns without contempt, and of the ancients without idolatry. Judge them all by their merits, whether old or new, and never stoop to the authority of any writer if your considerate judgment tells you that he is not to be trusted.

Some great scholars almost absurdly draw empiric maxims, both for public and private life, from what they call parallel cases in the ancient authors, without considering that in the first place, there never were two cases exactly parallel; and in the next place, there never was a case known—much less stated—with all its circumstances and conditions, by any historian. Wise saws and instances, ancient or modern, have undoubtedly great authority, but should be regarded rather as enforcements than proofs. Reason upon the case itself, taking into due consideration the circumstances and conditions. Look upon analogies as helps only, not as guides.

Whenever and wherever you are among those whose conversation is of an intellectual and exalted character, remember that a good listener is always a favorite. The art of listening well is sometimes preferable to the art of speaking well. Want of attention to a person who is speaking to you is a gross contravention of the law of politeness. It is a crime not easily pardoned by the victim, who feels it perhaps more keenly than an open insult. We know that towards " bores " it is almost impossible not to conduct one's self even with some marked show of inattention, but the well-bred man will rather seek the means of politely ridding himself of the " bore," and so have " one enemy the less," which is the next best to having " one friend the more." In listening to the conversation of another, it is not only necessary that you should attend, but that you should show your interest in the matter by frequent responses or ejaculations, or remarks. Passive silence merely, even with your eyes indicating attention, is not enough. You must show that you have been attending with your ears also, and that is best done by responding with your tongue.

One very common reason why we meet with so few people who are really agreeable in conversation is that there is scarcely anybody who does not think more of what he has to say, than of listening to and answering what is said to him. Even those who are reputed to have the greatest politeness sometimes think they do enough if they only *seem* to be attentive. At the same time their eyes and gestures betray a distraction as to what is addressed to them, and an impatience to return to what they themselves were saying. They forget that to be studious of pleasing themselves is but a poor way to please others, and that to listen patiently and answer complaisantly is essentially characteristic of good conversation. Without careful attention nothing can be done, and your attention should not only be careful and considerate, but quick and universal too, so far as your range is occupied, for where all are considered on an equality no one cares to be overlooked. Readiness of attention is also a valuable auxiliary to maintain that easy flow of conversation which is so liable to be interrupted by a change of speakers or of subjects. The fact is, that to be perfect in this, you should have within the range of your observation all that is transpiring around you —all the people, their motions, their looks, their words, and yet without staring at them or seeming to be an observer. Be ever ready for any little interchange of civility that may occur. Remember how pleased you were with the slightest mark of attention paid to you. The same result will follow when you show them to others.

Civility, it has been said, costs nothing, and yet it is of great value. We cannot dispense with the law to know all men. If a civil word or two will make a man happy, why should we withhold them when they cost us nothing. It is like "lighting another man's candle by one's own, which loses none of its light by what the other gains." A kind word or a kind action will often call forth more gratitude in the heart of the recipient than material benefits. It is quite possible for a man to be compelled to receive a benefit, and yet not thank the giver through the incivility of the conferment.

Be not forward in your deportment. Young persons should not assume consequence in any kind of society, but especially before men of age, wisdom and experience.

Boasting is a mode of putting one's self forward that is very offensive. Don't try it, for people won't believe a word of what you say. There's a good story told of a young clergyman in America boasting in company that he had been educated at two colleges, Harvard and Cambridge. "You remind me," said an aged divine present, "of an instance I knew of a calf that sucked two cows." "What was the consequence?" said a third person. "Why sir," replied the old gentleman very gravely, "the consequence was that he was a very *great calf*."

And in this connection we call attention to that very necessary characteristic—self respect. Though it has reference to self, it is a feeling that has nothing in common with boastfulness or egotism. The man who does not respect himself will never be respected by others. There is a dignity, in the assuming of which there is no arrogance but the greatest propriety. This dignity is quite compatible with modesty, hu-, mility, and all the unpretending virtues. It is a sad sight to see a man undervaluing himself and the purpose for which he was destined, by not employing, or by abusing the powers he possesses. One man fritters himself away in silly or ignoble pursuits; another helps to swell the current of crime by prostituting, it may be, splendid talents in the service of vice. Just think what a man is. Take Shakespeare's fine description—"What a piece of work is man! how noble in reason! how infinite in faculties! in form and moving how express and admirable! in action how like an angel! in apprehension how like a god!" It is quite right and proper to have an adequate idea of what you really are, and to act upon that idea, which you may very well do without arrogating more to yourself than is necessary. Self-respect, be it remembered, is acted not professed by word of mouth. Whenever you begin to talk of your self-respect you are in imminent danger of loosing it. He only can properly respect himself who orders all his thoughts and actions in accordance with the principles of religion and morality. It is nonsense to speak of a silly man or a bad man respecting himself. It is necessary to have the elements that cause respect to be entertained by others. The consciousness of having them and of ever acting on them induces the feeling in our breast. The meanest hind may be actuated by it as well as the proudest monarch. It is every man's safeguard against degradation. Whenever self-respect is gone, all trace of manliness is quickly lost.

Be careful to avoid the "loud laugh." It has been well described as speaking the "vacant mind." Loud laughter generally indicates a lamentable absence of due mental occupation. Whatever the truth of the matter may be, people generally suspect vacuity of thought "where laughter hath such room to ring," on the principle that "an empty barrel gives forth the greatest sound." You may laugh heartily yet not loudly nor noisily. "I have always preferred cheerfulness to mirth," says the essayist. It was the instinct of good manners that prompted the thought.

8

Cheerfulness produces the smile, and the gentle laugh, and fills the mind with the steady constant serenity of the summer day. Cheerfulness is the best mood for conversation. It is the most easily sustained and the most comfortably enjoyed. There are exceptions of course. Some by their flashes of wit can "set the table in a roar." Then the "roar" is proper and becoming, and the restraint of it would be pure affectation.

Unless a person has fairly brought down ridicule upon his own head, it is highly unbecoming to laugh at him. It destroys that sympathy without which no company can feel comfortable. Do not be too suspicious either that people are laughing at you. If you behave properly and people do laugh at you, it is to their own disadvantage, not yours.

A laugh may often be used judiciously in conversation to blunt the edge of some sarcasm that may have been ill-naturedly uttered against you. It shows that the barbed dart has not pierced your good nature and if you follow it up with a good-natured joke your victory is complete. The most detestable kind of laughter is the giggle—more so in man than in woman—and is the sure indication of not only vacuity of thought, but of lightness of intellect and instability of affection.

In the Family Circle.

It is the duty of every member of a family to do all he or she can to promote the happiness of the other members. It is necessary, therefore, to bear and forbear; to make mutual concessions; avoid selfishness; to rid ourselves of our petty likes and dislikes; to conquer and control our temper. Much may be done by a nice attention to the requirements of etiquette, by an observance of those laws which govern the decencies and proprieties of life. There is no reason why a husband should not treat his wife with exquisite politeness; why a wife should not remember that her husband has a claim to be treated like a gentleman; why the finest manners should not be observed by brothers and sisters. This mutual courtesy, inspired by mutual love, would purify the atmosphere of home, and invest with a new dignity our domestic relations. Let us make etiquette a matter of household concern. Why are we to throw off our politeness, like a cloak, when we cross our own threshold? Why should not our mother or sisters claim from us those graceful observances which we make it a point of honor to vouchsafe to strangers? The man who stands with his hat on in the presence of his mother and sister, manifests thereby such a want of apprehension of the requirements of filial and fraternal reverence and affection—of the rudiments of true domestic loyalty—as, if circumstances do not combine to correct him, will in the long-run render him fit for treason, stratagems, and spoils; he sets at naught feelings and principles which would interpose one of the most important barriers between himself and crime.

The happiness of home will be promoted by due attention to recreation. The heads of families should see that the younger members are provided with wholesome amusements. The cultivation of music and drawing, the reading aloud of good books, the introduction of a dance or a round game help wonderfully to facilitate the smooth passage of the hours. Too much cannot be said in praise of music. It is one of God's greatest gifts for making men happy. It is the only form in which we can express those thoughts and feelings which are too noble to be embodied in words, even in the words of the poets. It is the revelation of the inner harmonies of our spiritual nature. Carlyle calls it a kind of inarticulate, unfathomable speech, which leads us to the edge of the Infinite and lets us for moments gaze into that; but does any true lover of music believe it is, indeed, inarticulate? Unfathomable it may be, in the sense that we have not yet dived into all its meanings. Hence it is well that the cultivation of it enters into the ordinary curriculum of modern education. It is a great social instrument—to look at it in no higher light—and in the home circle its influence purifies, elevates, and strengthens. There will be no want of affection or confidence in the family where the young men and maidens help to make home happy in the evenings by their combined performances, their skilful blending of voices and instruments. A twofold harmony is created—a harmony outward and inward; a moral harmony as well as a harmony of sounds. Did you ever reflect what a void would be left in the world if music, or the art of it, could be forgotten? What would become of our pageants, our processions, our public welcomes of kings and statesmen? What would become of the pomp of royalty? How the martial array would suffer when not inspired by the strain and attuned to the measure of "flutes and recorders!" Where would be the awe and majesty, or the exultation and tenderness, of our religious services? All the charms of truth and pleasure would lose their joyance! Love would be denied its choicest vehicle of expression; mirth would be limited to laughter, which has but a poor faculty of significance. To lose the sublime swell and roll of the organ, which always seems to carry with it the mystery of the sea; to lose the ringing notes of the clarion; to lose the wonderful compass of the violin; to lose the blare of the trumpet and the liquid melody of the flute—ah! who can estimate the full extent of such a loss? The world without music would be a voiceless desert; life without music would be wanting in its purest inspiration.

Salutations.

In this country men do not embrace each other, nor do they exchange kisses, while, unless amongst intimate friends, even the fair sex now dispense with demonstrative salutations. In many European countries kisses are exchanged, even between gentlemen, and an embrace is quite in accordance with even a somewhat formal salutation. In America, however, these demonstrations are mostly confined to gushing misses and school-girls.

Men in this country acknowledge an introduction by extending the hand in greeting—the whole hand—for it is positively insulting to offer two fingers, as some under-bred snobs will sometimes do, and it is almost as bad to extend the left hand, unless two persons are introduced at the same time, or the right hand is useless or occupied; in any such case apologize for the hand extended. The right hand is the sword hand, and its extension to a friend is emblematic as a proof of peace, and as a safeguard against treachery.

In offering the hand to a friend in the house, always remove the glove, and grasp the hand given in return firmly for a moment. In the street, however, the glove may be retained, if it would cause an awkward pause to remove; but always in such a case apologize for the covered hand.

In shaking hands, do not try to wring them off the wrists, nor press them as in a vise, nor pull them as though they were bellhandles, nor fling the two together with violence, so as to cause a report. Let the palms grasp each other firmly, but without any display of energy, and shake the hand moderately for a moment, then release it. Mr. Pecksniff was wont to clasp his left hand over his " dear freind's " right hand, resting in his own right. This practice may be very effective, from a scenic point of view, but it is not countenanced by any rule of etiquette.

A lady must first recognize a gentleman by bowing before he is at liberty to salute her. She is the sole judge of the propriety of recognizing him at all, and etiquette requires the strictest deference to her desire in this respect. Should she recognize him, he should raise his hat a little from his head, with the hand furthest from her, and return her salutation with a slight inclination of the body. He may not obtrude himself upon her notice even if he thinks she has not observed him.

A lady should never stop in the street to salute a gentleman friend, nor may a gentleman join a lady in the street.

Should a lady, however, stop in meeting a gentleman, etiquette requires him to stop also, no matter how great his haste. If he is really unable to stop any time, he must at least pause long enough to state · this fact, and apologize for leaving her in such haste.

When a lady wishes to end a conversation in the street, she should bow slightly, and the gentleman must at once take his leave.

If a lady resumes her walk without any pause in the conversation, a gentleman is then at liberty to join her in her promenade.

Married ladies are allowed more freedom in such matters than unmarried ones. It is against all established laws of etiquette for young unmarried ladies to do more than bow to gentlemen in the street, unless the fact of relationship allows some violation of strict etiquette.

Unless related, or upon terms of intimate friendship with a gentleman, a lady should never salute excepting by a slightly formal bow. A nod is vulgar, even when exchanged by intimate friends.

In her own house, however, a lady should extend her hand in salutation to every guest who crosses her threshold.

Froissart, that charmingly quaint writer, tells of the dame of ancient days thus:

"When Sir Walter Manny and his men returned from a successfu sortie out of Henneboune, the chronicle tells us, 'The Countess d Montfort came down from the castle to meet them, and with a mos cheerful countenance kissed Sir Walter Manny and all his companions one after the other, like a noble and valiant dame.'" Modern etiquett would hardly speak in praise of such a lady in the current year.

On horseback a lady salutes by bowing slightly. A gentleman grasping reins and whip in his left hand, raises his hat slightly with hi right, at the same time inclining the body forward. He may not however, join a lady riding, unless she is escorted only by a groom and then he must first request permission to do so.

Never will a gentleman so far imitate a vulgar clown as to smack friend on the back, poke him in the ribs, or by clapping his hand upo his shoulder. It is equally bad taste to use a familiar shout, or "Hullo old boy!" or any other "Hail fellow, well met" phrase of salutation.

If a gentleman salutes another by mistake, even if he has given hin an unceremonious slap or poke, it is etiquette to treat the offender witl the utmost courtesy. He will probably be sufficiently embarrassed when he discovers his error, without having any blunt speech made t add to his discomfiture.

If a gentleman meet a gentleman, he may salute him by touching hi hat without removing it, but if a lady be with either gentleman botl hats must be lifted in salutation.

If a gentleman stops to speak to a lady in the street, he must hol his hat in his hand during the interview, unless she requests him t replace it. With a gentleman friend etiquette does not require thi formality.

A gentleman may bow to a lady seated at a window, if he is passin on the street, but he must not bow from a window to a lady on th street.

A gentleman may never offer to shake hands with a lady, but h must accept such an offer on her part, taking her hand lightly but firm ly in his ungloved right one, and delicately shaking it for a moment A pressure is an insult in such a case.

In entering a church a gentleman must remove his hat as soon as hi foot crosses the threshold of the sacred edifice. Travellers will ofter omit this salutation in visiting churches abroad, whose faith differs fron their own. There is no more certain sign of ill-breeding as well a irreverence.

A gentleman may always bow to a lady he may meet on a stairway even if not acquainted. If at the foot of the stairs, he must bow, pas her and ascend before her. If at the head of the stairs, he must bow, and wait for her to precede him in the descent.

If two friends are walking together and meet a friend of one, a bow is all the salutation etiquette demands; if, however, one of the two stops to speak to the third, he owes the friend he accompanies an apol ogy for the delay thus occasioned.

In entering a room, a gentleman must take his hat, cane and glove in his left hand leaving his right hand free for salutation.

If a 'gentleman, walking with a friend, meets a lady with whom hi
friend is acquainted, he must also bow, although the lady may be
stranger to him.   The bow must be very slight and formal, merely, i
fact, a compliment to his friend, and a mark of respect to the lady.

A gentleman must always return a bow made to him in the stree.
even if he fails to recognize the person who makes it.   It may be
person to whom he has been introduced, but whose face he has forgotter
and if it is an error on the part of the other, a courteous return of th;
salute will greatly diminish the embarrassment of the mistaken party.

In meeting a party of friends with some of whom you are intimatel·
acquainted, and with some only slightly, endeavor to make your salu
tations as equal as possible.   A formal bow to one, and a gushing
demonstration of delight over another is a breach of etiquette.   Be courteous and cordial to all.

If a foreigner salute you after the fashion of his own country, do not
draw back or allow yourself to smile, but strive to put him at his ease
by taking no notice of the "national salute."

Kissing in public, even between intimate lady friends, is a vulgar
parade of affection, that a truly refined person will shrink from.

It is an insult to return a cordial grasp of the hand, and hearty greeting, by a cold bow or a flabby extension of a portion of the hand.   Even
if you do not approve of the familiar greeting you should return it with
some show of cordiality.

The countess de ——, speaking of salutations, says:

"It would seem that good manners were originally the mere
expression of submission from the weaker to the stronger.   In a rude
state of society every salutation is to this day an act of worship.   Hence
the commonest acts, phrases and signs of courtesy with which we are
now familiar, date from those earlier stages when the strong hand ruled,
and the inferior demonstrated his allegiance by studied servility.   Let
us take for example the words 'Sir' and 'Madam.'   'Sir' is derived
from Seigneur, Sieur, Sire, and originally meant Lord, King, Ruler,
and in its patriarchal sense, Father.   The title of Sire was last borne
by some of the ancient feudal families of France who, as Selden has
said, 'affected rather to be styled by the name of Sire than Baron, as
Le Sire de Montmorenci and the like.'

"Madam or Madame, corrupted by servants into 'Ma'am,' and by
Mrs. Gamp and her tribe into 'Mum,' is in substance equivalent to
'Your exalted,' or 'Your Highness.'   *Ma Dame* originally meaning
high-born or stately, and being applied only to ladies of the highest
rank.

"To turn to our every-day forms of salutation.   We take off our hats
on visiting an acquaintance.   We bow on being introduced to strangers.   We rise when visitors enter our drawing-room.   We wave our
hand to our friends as he passes the window, or drives away from our
door.   The Oriental, in like manner, leaves his shoes on the threshold
when he pays a visit.   The natives of the Tonga Islands kiss the soles
of a chieftain's feet.   The Siberian peasant grovels in the dust before a
Russian noble.   Each of these acts has a primary, a historical signific-

ince.. The very word 'salutation' in the first place, derived as it is
from 'salutatio,' the daily homage paid by a Roman client to his patron,
suggests in itself a history of manners.

"To bare the head was originally an act of submission to gods and rulers.
A bow is a modified protestation. A lady's courtesy is a modified
genuflexion. Rising and standing are acts of homage; and when we
wave our hand to the friend on the opposite side of the street, we are
unconsciously imitating the Romans who, as Selden tells us, used to
stand 'somewhat off before the images of their gods, solemnly moving
the right hand to the lips and casting it as if they had cast kisses.'

"Again, men remove the glove when they shake hands with a lady—a
custom evidently of feudal origin. The knight removed his iron gauntlet, the pressure of which would have been all too harsh for the palm
of a fair *chatelaine*, and the custom which began in necessity has
travelled down to us as a point of etiquette."

General salutations of a mixed company are not now in vogue in the
best society, where etiquette requires that we recognize only our own
friends and acquaintances.

In meeting at a friend's house where you are visiting a circle who
are all entire strangers to you, remember that as mutual friends of the
host and hostess you are bound whilst under the same roof to consider
yourselves as acquaintances. No spirit of exclusiveness is an apology
for a neglect of this, and no shyness can excuse a withdrawing into a
corner, a clinging to one friend alone in such a circle.

Baptisms.

In the baptisms of infants there are certain customs in the world of
good society, independent of the religious ceremonies. A few hints
will suffice, as each sect has its own peculiar forms known to the
members of that church; we do not profess to guide these, but merely
the worldly observances.

It is not customary to invite mere acquaintances to be godfather or
godmother to an infant; these should be tried friends of long standing,
or better still, near relations, to whom the obligations thus imposed
will be pleasures and not tasks.

Never invite any friends to be godfather or godmother, who are not
of the same church as the child to be baptized.

When you are invited to stand godfather or godmother to an infant,
never refuse without grave cause, and then do so immediately, that the
parents may have time to make other arrangements.

It is unkind, as well as impolite, to refuse to act in this capacity
towards children who, from poverty or other reasons, may occupy an
inferor position in society to your own.

It is customary to allow the godmother to select herself the godfather.

It is, however, customary for the maternal grandmother and the paternal grandfather to act as sponsors for the first child; the paternal grandmother and the maternal grandfather as sponsors for the second child. If the grand-parents are not living, the nearest relatives of the same church should be invited.

It is customary for the sponsors to make the babe a present If it is a little boy, the godfather gives a silver cup, with the full name engraved upon it, and the godmother some pretty piece of silver, jewelry, or dress. If a little girl, it is the godmother who gives the cup, and the godfather the other gift. Where the sponsors are wealthy, it is not unusual to fill the christening-cup with gold pieces. The godmother often adds to her gift the christening robe and cap, both trimmed with white ribbons—for a babe should wear only pure white when presented for baptism.

It is contrary to etiquette to invite young persons to stand as sponsors for an infant.

In the Roman Catholic church, it is customary to baptize an infant as soon as possible. If the child is very delicate, it is customary to send at once for the priest, and have the ceremony performed in the bedroom; but if the babe is healthy and likely to live, it is usually taken to the church for baptism, as young as the physician will permit.

In entering the church, the nurse, carrying the child, goes first; then follow the sponsors, who do not walk arm-in-arm; then the father, and after him the invited guests.

When the ceremony commences, the sponsors stand on each side of the child, the godfather on the right, and the godmother on the left.

The babe should be held lying in the arms of the nurse, its head upon the right arm. The cap should be tied so as to be easily unfastened and removed.

When the priest asks who are the sponsors of the child, it is sufficient for them to incline the head, without speaking.

Baptism is a gratuitous ceremony in the church, but it is customary for the father to present some token to the officiating clergyman, in the name of the babe, or, where parents are wealthy, to make a handsome donation to the poor of the parish, through the clergyman.

In the Protestant churches, it is customary to defer the baptism until the mother of the child can be present.

It is always desirable to have the ceremony performed in the church, if possible; but if there is a necessity for it, such as the illness of the child or the parents, it can take place in the house of the parents, by their special request.

No one should ever offer to act as sponsor for a child. It is the privilege of the parents to make the selection amongst their relatives or friends.

If the ceremony is performed at the house of the parents, a carriage must be sent to the house of the clergyman to convey him to the house of the parents, and wait until after the ceremony, to convey him home again. It is extremely rude to expect a clergyman to provide his own conveyance, or to walk.

Friends invited to a christening usually carry some gift to the babe; gentlemen a gift of silver, and ladies some pretty piece of needlework.

If the ceremony is performed in the house of the parents, or if the guests return there from the church, the only refreshments required by etiquette are cake and wine.

The father of the child usually gives a present of money to the nurse who carries the babe to the church.

It is not etiquette to remain long at a christening; and it is better taste for the infant to be removed to the nursery as soon as the ceremony is over. To keep a weary mother sitting up entertaining guests, or a cross, tired child on exhibition, are either of them in bad taste.

For a guest to show any annoyance if a child cries loudly, or is in any way troublesome, is the height of rudeness. Remarks or even frowns are forbidden entirely, even if the infant screams so as to make the voice of the clergyman entirely inaudible.

Etiquette requires that the babe be praised if it is shown to the guests, even if it is a little monster of pink ugliness. Ladies, especially mothers, will *see* something beautiful, if only its helpless innocence, and gentlemen must behold infantile graces, if they cannot actually behold them. "Mother's darling" must be the great attraction at a christening, if it only improves the occasion by a succession of yells.

In Church.

In visiting a church in which you have no pew of your own, wait in the vestibule until the sexton comes to you, and request him to show you to a seat. It is extremely rude to enter a pew without invitation if it is partially filled, or without permission if it is empty.

Always enter a church slowly and reverentially. A gentleman must remove his hat at the door, and never replace it until he is again in the vestibule.

Conform strictly to the forms of worship. If you are not familiar with them, rise, kneel, and sit as you see others do.

Never whisper to a companion in church.

Never make any noise with your feet or fingers.

Never stare round the building.

Never bow to any friend while in the church itself. Greetings may be exchanged in the vestibule after service.

A gentleman accompanying a lady to a Roman Catholic church, even if himself a Protestant, may offer her the holy water, and it must be with an ungloved hand.

Gentlemen must pass up the aisle beside their lady companions until they reach the pew, then advance a few steps, open the door, and stand aside until she has entered, then enter, and close the door again. It is a bad plan to leave the hat outside, as it is liable to be swept down the aisle by the skirts of ladies passing. If there is not room for it on the seat, it can be put upon the floor inside the pew.

Never pay any attention to those around you, even if they are noisy or rude.

If you pass a book or a fan to a person in the same pew, or accept the same attention, it is not necessary to speak. A silent bow is all that etiquette requires.

If you have room in your own pew, and see a stranger enter, open the door and motion him to enter. It is not necessary to speak.

You may find the place and point it out to a stranger, who is unfamiliar with the service; but do so silently.

A lady should never remove her gloves in church, unless to use the holy water, or the right-hand glove at communion.

To come late to church is not only ill-bred, but disrespectful. It is equally so to hurry away, or to commence preparations for departure, closing and putting away the books, and such preparations, before the service closes.

Never keep any one waiting if you are invited or have invited them to go to church.

When visiting a church abroad, not to attend divine service, but to see the edifice, choose an hour when there is no service. If you find worshippers, however, are present, move quietly, speak low, and endeavor not to disturb their devotions.

The godmother at a christening must accompany the family of her little godchild to and from the church, and should send her gift (usually a silver cup) the day before.

In attending a funeral not in your own family, never leave the pew until the mourners have passed into the aisle; but rise and stand while they pass, falling into your proper place as the procession passes you.

It is ill-bred for gentlemen to congregate in the vestibule of a church and there chat familiarly, often commenting audibly upon the service or the congregation. No true lady likes to run this gauntlet, although in this country they are too often obliged to do so.

To show any disrespect to a form of worship that may be new or strange to you is rude in the extreme. If you find it trying to your own religious convictions, you need not again visit churches of the same denomination; but to sneer at a form, while in the church using that form, is insulting and low-bred.

With Children.

It is against the rules of etiquette to take a child when making formal calls, as they are a restraint upon conversation, even if they are not troublesome about touching forbidden articles, or teasing to go home.

Never take a child to a funeral, either to the house of mourning or to the cemetery.

Never allow a child to take a meal at a friend's house without special invitation. It is impossible to know how much she may be inconvenienced, while her regard for the mother would deter her from sending the little visitor home again.

Never allow a child to handle goods in a store,

Never send for children to meet visitors in the drawing-room, unless the visitors themselves request to see them. Make their stay then very brief, and be careful that they are not troublesome.

Never take a child to church until it is old enough to remain perfectly quiet. Although you may be accustomed to its restless movements, and not disturbed by them, others near you will certainly feel annoyed by them.

It is not etiquette to put a child to sleep in the room of a guest, nor to allow children to go at all to a guest's room, unless especially invited to do so, and even then to make long stay there.

Etiquette excludes children from all companies given to grown persons, from all parties and balls, excepting such as are given especially for their pleasure.

When invited to walk or drive, never take a child, unless it has been invited, or you have requested permission to do so; even in the latter case, the consent is probably given more from good-nature than from any desire to have a juvenile third to the party.

Never crowd children into pic-nic parties, if they have not been invited. They generally grow weary and very troublesome before the day is over.

Never take a child to spend the day with a friend unless it has been included in the invitation.

Never allow children to be in the drawing-room if strangers are present.

Never allow children to handle the ornaments in the drawing-room of a friend.

Never allow a child to pull a visitor's dress, play with the jewelry or ornaments she may wear, take her parasol or satchel for a plaything, or in any way annoy her.

Train children early to answer politely when addressed, to avoid restless, noisy motions when in company, and gradually inculcate a love of the gentle courtesies of life. By making the rules of etiquette habitual to them, you remove all awkwardness and restraint from their manners when they are old enough to go into society.

Never send a child to sit upon a sofa with grown people, nnless they express a desire to have it do so.

Never crowd a child into a carriage seat between two grown people.

Never allow a child to play with a visitor's hat or cane.

If children are talented, be careful you do not weary your friends, and destroy their own modesty by "showing them off," upon improper occasions. What may seem wonderful to an interested mother, may be an unutterable weariness to a guest, too polite to allow the mother to perceive the incipient yawn.

Never allow children to visit upon the invitation of other children. When they are invited by the older members of the family, it is time to put on their "best bibs and tucker."

Never take children to a house of mourning, even if you are an intimate friend.

The custom for having children in the drawing-room for morning or evening parties, or in the dining-room with the dessert at dinner companies, is not only often an annoyance to the guests, but bad for the children themselves.

It is one of the first duties of parents to train their children at home as they would have them appear abroad. An English lady writes thus :

"If, then, we desire that our children shall become ladies and gentlemen, can we make them so, think you, by lavishing money upon foreign professors, dancing-masters, foreign travel, tailors, and dressmakers? Ah, no! good breeding is far less costly, and begins far earlier than those things. Let our little ones be nurtured in an atmosphere of gentleness and kindness from the nursery upwards; let them grow up in a home where a rude gesture or an ill-tempered word are alike unknown; where between father and mother, master and servant, mistress and maid, friend and friend, parent and child, brother and sister, prevails the law of truth, of kindness, of consideration for others, and forgetfulness of self. Can they carry into the world, whither we send them later, aught of coarseness, of untruthfulness, of slatternliness, of vulgarity, if their home has been orderly, if their parents have been refined, their servants well mannered, their friends and playmates kindly and carefully trained as themselves? Do we want our boys to succeed in the world; our girls to be admired and loved; their tastes to be elegant; their language choice; their manners simple, charming, refined, and graceful; their friendship elevating? then we must ourselves be what we would have our children to be, remembering the golden maxim, that good manners, like charity, must begin at home.

"Good manners are an immense social force. We should, therefore, spare no pains to teach our children what to do, and what to avoid doing, in their pathway through life.

"On utilitarian as well as social principles, we should try to instruct our children in good manners; for whether we wish them to succeed in the world, or to adorn society, the point is equally important. We must never lose sight of the fact, that here teachers and professors can do little, and that the only way in which it is possible to acquire the habits of good society is, to live in no other."

Games with Cards.

Married ladies and elderly gentlemen are allowed to claim precedence at the card-table, over single young ladies and the younger men. Ladies of "a certain age," if single, can claim the privileges of the card-table with married ladies.

Etiquette does not require any one to play unwillingly. It is very rude to urge the request, as many have conscientious scruples on this matter, though they may not care to wound the feelings of those playing by proclaiming them.

It is not kind, however, and therefore it is not etiquette, to refuse to play, if there are no such scruples, when the refusal prevents a game being made up.

None should attempt to play—whist, for instance—unless really able to do so moderately well. It is not fair to impose a poor partner upon one who may be really fond of the game and play well.

It is not etiquette for those very fond of card-playing to victimize every guest by producing cards whenever they call, whether they care for playing or not. Many will play from good-nature who would prefer to pass the time in conversation.

Husband and wife, or any partners who may be supposed to be intimately acquainted with each other's play, should not play together. It is taking an unfair advantage of the other couple for them to play partners.

If playing for stakes, the gentleman pays for his lady partner in the event of loss; but does not receive her winnings.

All violations of the known rules of the game are violations of the laws of etiquette as well. Yet, if such violations are made, they should be pointed out in a quiet and courteous manner, not made the subject of violent dispute or censure. Any altercations are violations of the laws of etiquette. Loss of temper, no matter how continuous the ill-luck, is a breach of manners; so are objurgations of one's partner's performances, and criticisms on the play of partner or adversary. In whist, as in marriage, the partner is taken for better for worse, and in neither case should an ill-assorted couple try to make matters worse than they are by grumbling and growling at each other.

It is a breach of etiquette to talk constantly upon other subjects whilst engaged in a game of cards. Whist, as all good players know, is a game that requires close attention, and almost absolute silence; and the other games can be much disturbed by talking.

To converse with those who are not playing is still worse. It is a violation of all courtesy to allow the attention to be diverted at all. If addressed while at the game, make your answer as brief as politeness will permit, and give your whole attention to the game again. No one can play so well with divided attention; and you may be certain it is an annoyance to your partner, even if your opponent does not object to it.

Any appearance of an understanding between partners, as smiles, nods, or winks, are gross violations, not only of the laws of the game, but of good manners.

To finger the cards whilst they are being dealt, is a breach of good manners. Even if you do not violate the laws of the game by actually looking at them, you are committing an error in etiquette by seeming to be in any way aware of their existence before you are at liberty to take them in your hand.

Never start a conversation that would lead to long argument or discussion in the pauses of the game. Small talk, chit-chat, is certainly admissible whilst the cards are being dealt, but only upon topics which can be readily dropped when the play is again the leading subject.

- To play cards with an air of weariness or abstraction is positively rude. If you are interested in the game, strive to appear so, and if you are not equal to that, you had better stop playing.

Try to avoid argument upon nice points in playing. Even if you are right, it is more courteous to your adversary than to keep others waiting whilst you prove your position.

Etiquette by no means requires stakes of money. If counters are not provided for betting games, you may refuse to bet, without any breach of good manners.

In your own house, never offer guests any but *new* cards to play with.

It is a violation of etiquette to propose card-playing in another person's house. This is the privilege of the host or hostess, and if they do not suggest the amusement, it is absolutety rude for any one else to do so.

It is a breach of etiquette to hurry others who are playing. Nothing annoys a deliberate player more than to have a partner or adversary constantly saying, "Come, play; it is your turn now," or, "We are all waiting for you."

Even if you take no pleasure in cards, some knowledge of the etiquette and rules belonging to the games most in vogue will be useful to you, unless you object upon principle to playing. If so, it is better at once to state the fact. If not, and a fourth hand is wanted at a rubber, or if the rest of the company sit down to a round game, you will be deemed guilty of a want of politeness if you refuse to join.

The games most common are whist, loo, euchre, vingt-un and speculation, to which may be added poker, which of late years has become very popular in all circles.

Whist requires four players. A pack of cards being spread upon the table, with their faces downward, the four players draw for partners. Those who draw the two highest and those who draw the two lowest, become partners. The lowest of all claims the deal.

In declaring that married people may not play at the same table, society by no means understands anything so disgraceful as dishonest collusion; but persons who play regularly together cannot fail to know so much of each other's mode of acting under given circumstances that the chances no longer remain perfectly even in favor of their adversaries.

Good Taste.

In the various preceding topics we have endeavored to give a detail of personal quality and manner; but these will not form the power that is necessary to produce them. That power is the working of a principle, and this principle is to be found in the self-moving power of the mind to guide itself along the road of life, in obedience to the laws made by its Maker. We do not want you to be made up of patchwork, or of clockwork, or of anything artificial—we wish you to be the power in your mind that acts in your manner as the law of true politeness demands. All that you are in your mind passes off into the world through your acts, the manner of which is found to have as much positive influence as the matter—from which, however, it derives originally all its force. Look at the difference between an elegant and powerful, and a blundering, impotent speaker. The former can polish falsehood into a seeming truth, whilst the latter bedims and bedarkens the clearest axioms until they become as opaque as a mill-stone. In fact, we would wish you to be what you would seem to be, and then you will have little trouble and much pleasure in seeming to be. It is not only the true thing, but the most effective and the most pleasant thing. We take you to be young, and ambitious of showing that you are worth something. You are desirous not only of a standing in society, but ambitious of influencing that society in a manner creditable and pleasant to yourself; but would scorn to stoop to unworthy means to attain your end. In all probability, then, you have received a good average education, that will form a good ground-work for your endeavor. As thinking, with its processes and its modes, though in itself the process of education so far as the mind is concerned, is seldom or never taken into account at school, except in so far as it cannot be done without, even to have done what is done, you will have to begin, if you have not done so before, to study this the great instrument of life in all its adaptations. The best thinkers are the best workmen of life. These are the men who carve time into money—not the best use of it, however, but a use very potent with some. This, however, has to do with the morality of thought, and at present we have to do with the power. In all probability the real solid power of your education is now about to be formed and directed to legitimate issues. Energy and perseverance are required, and a good deal of self-denial. Set your face steadily against the small pleasures of the world that entice the precious time from you bit by bit. Set about your endeavor with the consciousness of an unavoidable responsibility. The business of life now in all likelihood claims the greater part of your time. This is the time you are compelled by your necessities to convert into money; but you may at the same time convert it in something more—something that will last when your money is gone. Contact with the world in transacting your business will sharpen your powers and polish your manner, if you submit yourself to the process with proper aims and discriminating judgment. There is a worry in business, however, which merely grinds without polishing, which ought to be avoided if possible. Otherwise the cheerful intercourse of business should fit a man more and more to "shine" substantially and decidedly. If truth be your ideal, as it ought to be, the veracity of your conversation and the honesty of your dealings will win you respect and attention; but in addition it is necessary that you cultivate elegance of taste in order to win you favor.

This elegance of taste, or the appreciation of what is beautiful in matter or manner, is the polishing principle that will enable you to shine truly. You may be a diamond of the first water, yet if you do not cut and polish and set yourself with this æsthetic instrument, you may coruscate, scintillate, or flash forth light at any rate, but it will be fitful, temporary, and unsustained, and ever out of keeping and proportion with itself. Now what do you do with your leisure hours? Here is an opportunity for you to spend them pleasantly, profitably, and dutifully in the highest sense of the term.

A love for the beautiful is natural to man, so there is a natural pleasure in the pursuit of it, and all cultivate an acquaintance with it more or less. Conversation glowing with it is sure to fascinate in proportion to the amount and power of the quality. This indeed is the true beautifier of all conversation. A memory teeming with knowledge and an intellect beaming with thought may arrest and impress with respect, but it is the genial fancy that beautifies with light, warmth, and color, which charms and captivates. Now the best drill for attaining this power in conversation is the culture of it. It takes a deal of practice to attain a power, so do not be discouraged if the power does not come so soon as desired. Besides, this one original power, if you acquire it, will help to form originality in all other acquirements you may have. Originality is the soul of all power. Originality does not mean that you create a power yourself unlike any other in creation. It means that you have formed for yourself a power in nature, in conformity with the laws of nature in and around you. You have thus a power to produce for yourself, which, if you have it not, you will be forced to derive, not in itself but in its effects, from others. Try to attain original not derivative ornament, and so avoid the imputation of the jack-daw in the peacock's feathers. This is not the place to give an analysis of the process of drill. We have space only to point out the great importance and the influence of the power. It may not be out of place, however, to give a few hints as to the method by which it may be acquired.

This power is but the refinement of the other powers of the mind, and will be weak or strong in proportion to them. This is the power that makes the other powers shine, or rather it is the power of thought and the sense of feeling polished so that they shine. In the words of the old Greek critic, "it is the image reflected from the inward beauty of the soul." The mind you form by your education stamps the character of your soul, and what your soul is, that only can your manner be. Nor need you lament want of education. If you can read, and set yourself seriously to think, a world of teachers may be had for a very little money. Remember that self-education is the only real education, and at the best universities if the students do not educate themselves they are not really educated. The best part of those institutions is the routine and method and discipline enforced. We do not desire, however, to depreciate those conservatories of learning, we only wish to impress you who have not the means nor the opportunity, that you can do very well without them. There is a university for the million in literature, and the "humanities" are now freed from the Latin and Greek tongues. The best teachers will instruct you, the best lecturers will read to you by your own fireside, but you, on your part, must cultivate the power of thinking and the habit of study. The living voice to be sure is no longer there to thrill with enthusiasm, and undoubtedly if you have the means and opportunity you should get a living instructor whose soul will come into living contact with your own.

In this wonderful world there are many fields of inquiry open to you wherein you may gather for yourself materials for exercising your powers of thought, but there is one in which every one must adopt a sphere of labor, and wherein he may gather ample materials for the purposes of thought, and that is humanity. What we term pure literature is the record of it, and it is ever living round about us, and continually coming into contact with us.

Useful knowledge may now be gleaned under the most favorable circumstances in consequences of the vast harvests that are continually being gathered in. A cheap printing press—cheap on account of the extent of the demand for its treasures—sends the wisest and most learned teachers to instruct the poorest respectable man. It rests with himself to make his knowledge and wisdom not only useful but ornamental. There is more true knowledge at the present day in our shops and counting-houses than there was of old in the most learned universities. Facts are infinitely more useful than the subtlest distinctions of imputed qualities, labored disquisitions on possible entitles, and interminable logomachies. Classic Latin and scholastic logic "are nowhere," compared with our own simple vernacular English and common sense. Make physical science or the knowledge of facts the whetstone of your mind, and polish it into refinement with literature. Physics may be studied at any of our mechanics' institutions for a fee merely nominal, so that none who have any pretensions at all to the improvement of their minds labor under difficulties of means and opportunities which they cannot surmount. The finest results have been attained by the simplest means.

Nothing makes a greater difference between people engaged in conversation than different degrees and methods of knowledge. An ignorant person, if he knows his own ignorance, can at least begin to learn, and so be in the way of improving, but often his greatest ignorance is that he does not know his own ignorance, and this is a hopeless case indeed. Of course, if a man, however learned, takes himself to task about his own positive knowledge, he will find himself not so learned as he thought, and after such an ordeal he is apt to say that he is really but an ignorant person at the best, but still he knows something, however little that be; and that little is a great deal compared with the knowledge of a person who has bestowed no attention at all upon the subject. We should always hold ourselves capable of learning by cultivating the disposition to do so, and then we shall feel astonished at our ability to understand the most difficult questions that may come before us.

Wrong headedness is a worse state of mind than absolute ignorance. It may almost be called a modified type of madness. A chaos of ideas must result in confusion of thought and unwise action. This arises from slovenliness and want of method in thinking. A person who allows himself to fall into such a state, and to contract so idle and hurtful a habit, can never meet with respect in the interchange of social converse. This is what the poet Burns called "an in-kneed sort of a soul."

The man learning, whose knowledge has been arranged by systematic method so that he can produce it at will when required, produces a current of conversation that flows clearly and pleasantly, especially when that knowledge is made to bear the precious burthen of wise and beautiful thoughts.

Of course the end we aim at here—to be a tolerably well informed gentleman so that one may occupy a not undignified position in the social circle—is not the only nor the highest aim achieved, though the one more immediately sought for at present. The higher aim we have throughout kept in view is one never to be relinquished for a present and merely transient good.

With regard to advice as to what should form specially the subject of studies, the following words of Thomas Carlyle are much to the point. A young friend had written to him for advice on the subject, and was answered thus:—"It would give me true satisfaction could any advice of mine contribute to forward you in your honorable course of self-improvement, but a long experience has taught me that advice can profit but little; that there is a good reason why advice is so seldom followed; this reason, namely, that it is so seldom, and can almost never be rightly given. No man knows the state of another; it is always to some more or less imaginary man that the wisest and most honest adviser is speaking

"As to the books which you—whom I know so little of—should read, there is hardly anything definite that can be said. For one thing, you may be strenuously advised to keep reading. Any good book, any book that is wiser than yourself, will teach you something—a great many things, indirectly and directly if your mind be open to learn. This old counsel of Johnson's is also good, and universally adplicable: 'Read the book that you do honestly feel a wish and curiosity to read.' The very wish and curiosity indicate that you, then and there, are the person likely to get good of it. 'Our wishes are presentiments of our capabilities;' that is a noble saying, of deep encouragement to all true men; applicable to our wishes and efforts in regard to reading, as to other things. Among all the objects that look wonderful or beautiful to you, follow with fresh hope one that looks wonderfullest, beautifullest. You will gradually find, by various trials—which trials see that you make honest, manful ones, not silly, short, fitful ones—what *is* for you the wonderfullest, beautifullest, what is *your* true element and province, and be able to profit by that.

"All books are properly the record of the history of past men, what thoughts past men had in them, what actions past men did; the summary of all books whatsoever lies there. It is on this ground that the class of books specifically named History, can be safely recommended as the basis of all study of books— the preliminary to all right and full understanding of anything we can expect to find in books. Past history, and especially the past history of one's native country, everybody may be advised to begin with that. Let him study that faithfully; innumerable inquiries will branch out from it. He has a broad beaten highway, from which all the country is more or less visible; there travelling, let him choose where he will dwell.

"Neither let mistakes and wrong directions—of which every man, in his studies and elsewhere falls into many—discourage you. There is precious instruction to be got by finding that we are wrong. Let a man try faithfully, manfully, to be right; he will grow daily more and more right. It is, at bottom, the condition on which all men have to cultivate themselves. Our very walking is an incessant falling; a falling and a catching of ourselves before we come actually to the pavement!" It is emblematic of all things a man does.

"In conclusion, I will remind you that it is not by books alone, or by books chiefly, that a man becomes in all points a man. Study to do faithfully whatsoever thing in your actual situation, there and now, you find either expressly or tacitly laid to your charge; that is your post; stand in it like a true soldier. Silently devour the many chagrins of it, as all human situations have many; and see you aim not to quit it without doing all that it, at least, required of you. A man perfects himself by work much more than by reading. They are a growing kind of men that can wisely combine the two things—wisely, valiantly, can do what is laid to their hand in their present sphere, and prepare themselves withal for doing other wider things, if such lie before them."

All this advice is sterling wisdom, and of infinite value to the man who wishes to form the power we are desirous he should form within himself. A man who moulds himself so, will have force and energy of his own, which will make itself felt in whatever sphere he may find himself. But attend more specially in the meantime to that part of the advice in which he says: "Among all the objects that look wonderful or beautiful to you, follow with fresh hope, the one that looks wonderfullest, beautifullest."

"Walk with the beautiful and with the grand,
Let nothing on the earth thy feet deter:
Sorrow may lead thee moping by the hand,
But give not all thy bosom thoughts to her.
Walk with the beautiful.

"I hear thee say 'The beautiful! What is it?'
Oh, thou art darkling ignorant—be sure
'Tis no long weary road its form to visit,
For thou can'st make it smile beside thy door,
Then love the beautiful.

"Thy bosom is its mint, the workmen are
Thy thoughts, and they must coin for thee;
The beautiful is master of a star,
Thou mak'st it so, but art thyself deceiving
If otherwise thy faith."

Yes; the beautiful is coin that shining fresh from the mint of your thoughts in conversation will dazzle and fascinate the receivers, and will win favor and reputation for the coiner and distributor. The culture of the beautiful in thought and expression, is the finishing polish to all the other solid acquirements and abilities of your mind and manner. The beautiful is the irresistible and the invincible. We now proceed to give a few hints on the acquirement of this valuable state of thought and feeling.

We do not mean that you are to get up the power of talking the beautiful so as to shine amidst your compeers, and eclipse them by your beautiful talk. We mean you so to steep your powers in an ever present consciousness of the beautiful, so that it may pervade your entire being, and settle down into the habitual exercise of a good and elegant taste.

For this purpose it is not necessary that you enter into a metaphysical study of the beautiful, wherein you may get bewildered and lost in attempting to find some ideal standard. Study it as you would the true and the good—study it along with these, and your perception will not readily fail to see it when it is present.

This faculty extends to such a variety of subjects that there is hardly a phase of your conduct not affected by it. Take the example of color. How much does a due appreciation of fitness in harmony or contrast affect your personal appearance in the matter of dress. By that alone will your claim to elegant taste be judged by society. See what a difference between the uncultured taste of the country bumpkin, the fashionable taste of the city swell, and the cultured refinement of the thorough gentleman. Again, in the matter of sound, what a vast difference between the ungoverned, because untrained, voice of the blustering talker, and the obedient, pliant, mellow bell-tone of the elegant speaker. The former rends the air with dissonance, and our hearts discord; the latter with persuasive pathos floats through our charmed ears into our assenting and consenting hearts.

With regard to beauty of form, we presume much need not be said, as all are aware how powerful it is in its effects. We have little control over the form that nature has given us except by modifying its appearance, but even that is a good deal under our control. We do not appear in society as nature has turned us out of her hands. We pass through the hands of the barber, the tailor, the shoemaker, the hatter, etc., and we pass a good deal through our hands daily. In all these modifications of nature there is wide room for the excercise of an elegant taste, or the contrary.

As a matter of course all the several possible modifications of what is elegant and tasteful come under the common term of what is elegant in thought and in feeling. The several manifestations of taste are but the expression of these outwardly, and derive all their truth and beauty and propriety of effect from the genuine power and quality of these as they exist and are developed in the mind.

The power and the habit are best obtained by the formal pursuit of some art-study, as the composition and expression of thought in prose or verse, the art of drawing or painting, or some study which takes you into the habitual presence of the beautiful—in fact, any pursuit that makes you think continuously regarding that wonderful beautiful arrangement of things which made the old Greeks call the world by the same term they had to express beauty.

There is one sphere of good taste more suited to those for whom we are writing than any other, and that is the culture of good taste in thought and feeling through the habitual culture of it in our literature, and even the literary culture of it in written expression. "Reading," says Bacon, "maketh a full man, conference a ready man, and writing an exact man." By perusing the elegent in literature, the fine taste will impregnate your thoughts till you become full of it. By talking the elegance over with your associates you will the more readily make them subservient to your own refinement; but only by bringing them to a strict scrutiny and account with your own pen will you make their influence felt and their nature and effects definite and exact. You have not at all times friends willing and ready enough to talk matters over, but whenever you please you may take up your pen or your pencil, and bring yourself or your thoughts to book. Thinking or even talking a matter over is vapory in its results compared with writing it over. And then writing comprehends all other particular modes, for it comprehends all that is in thought. There is no pursuit that will react on your conversation like writing. Remember, however, it is not writing for others but for yourself. There is a mawkish sentimentality about writing which is most pernicious. No sooner does one mention writing than there rises up the absurd notion of "turning author." As well link the idea of "turning spouter" with the art of speech. In these days everybody should possess the art of writing as well as the arts of reading and speaking, and of doing it well too. Ay—and even the art of versifying should not be neglected with supercilious scorn and contempt as it is by cotton-hearted money-makers, for as by learning to dance, we gain grace to the motion as we walk, so by causing our words to move in numbers, we gain elasticity and elegance to the rhythm of our prose. This reproducing of the elegant in our own words tends to consolidate and establish our habit of thinking in good taste, and acting in good taste is only one step farther, and the former must be had before the latter can be taken.

Thought and behavior are so intimately related that you can hardly cultivate elegance in the former, without a corresponding result in the latter. There is no reason for a hypocrisy in this, and so the thought will naturally reveal itself in the manner. Again, behavior can only sustain itself consistently when it flows from an ever-springing fount of thought. That fount derives its spring from the depths of a large experience, on which have fallen the dews and showers of many readings and studyings and thinkings. Tennyson finely and truly says,

> "For who can *always act* but *he*
> To whom a *thousand memories* call?"

A man's memories shower upon him inducements that compel him to act; the remembered thoughts are the potent ones, and the earnestly acted ones.

You see that conversation is not limited to talking merely—it embraces your general conduct as well. The tongue indeed has a wonderful empire of its own, but it merely produces the echo of the thought, on which it depends for its force and its beauty. But the behavior is the expression of the man, and the impression made comes from the more effective stamp of the entire earnest character.

To be able to surround yourself and others in the social circle with delight and happiness is surely to have the power of shining to advantage in a most legitimate and most delightful way. But this will depend in a great measure on the associates of your thoughts. Are you content to choose these from those of common-place quality, or from those which are ever found in the highest places—the palaces of thought?

Observe then that the transmutation of your coarser metal into finer, and the refinement of that into finer still, is done within the laboratory of your brain, and here it is that you must work out the process of knowing "how to shine" with a true and becoming lustre. You have, moreover, every inducement to make yourself at home in this, happy and contented, for it is about the pleasantest occupation a man can be engaged in, and deepens and broadens and brightens, day after day spent upon it, our personal pleasure and happiness. Real and imaginary pleasures are very often confounded. In the testing laboratory of real thought, what is supposed to be real pleasure often changes into a solution of vanity with a pale precipitate of sorrow; and what appears to be purely imaginary becomes a durable and lasting—sometimes everlasting —solid. There is a misnamed elegant taste in the world, which is a vitiated and corrupted one. A man may have what is really capable of yielding a result, and yet may not be able to make it yield it to him; he may not have the wisdom to extract or distil, though he may have the material. Of course he must have the material to be able to perform the process; but the process is quite a distinct thing from the material, and you may buy the material, but you cannot buy your own act of the process—that is entirely a personal thing. But the rights of property in this matter of taste are vested only in those who can use them, not merely in those who possess them, so that this beautiful little world is ever open to those who choose to enter in and possess it. Hazlitt humorously and somewhat truly describes this in the following racy description:—"When I am in the country, all the seats near the place of my residence, and to which I have access, I regard as mine. The same I think of the groves and fields where I walk, and muse on the folly of the civil landlord in London, who has the fantastical pleasure of draining dry rents into his coffers, but is a stranger to the fresh air and rural enjoyments. By these principles I am possessed of half-a-dozen of the finest seats in England, which, in the eye of the law, belong to certain of my acquaintances, who, being men of business, choose to *live near the court.*" Is not this true and real enjoyment without the troubles and anxieties that detract from the pleasure, which the possessor necessarily has in the owning, and the maintenance of the ownership?

" In some great families," naively continues Hazlitt, "where I choose to pass my time, a stranger would be apt to rank me with the other domestics; but, in my own thoughts and natural judgment, I am master of the house, and he who goes by that name is my steward, who eases me of the care of providing for myself the conveniences and pleasures of life." Though quiet, what satire could be more pungent on the folly of thinking we are happy and enjoying life, if we are master of a splendid establishment, ornamented to the full with magnificent display. To those born in, and born to, high life, what splendid misery to be born to such as mere necessities of existence; and to those born in humble lite, but to whose unremitting exertions, high life, the beacon of all their toiling hopes, has at length come as the crowning reward, what splendid disappointment and sorrow to attempt, with daily failure, to crush some sweet out of the daily glitter and the show! What is not in them cannot be taken out of them. What is sought after is in the refinement of the mind, and may be had without them—at least without paying for them in false circumstance or a lifetime of slavery.

How exquisitely does he continue his good humored satire in the following, and notice that he speaks from a conscious possession of the very power we wish you to have:—"When I walk the streets I use the foregoing natural maxim, namely,—that he is the true possessor of a thing who enjoys it, and not he that owns it, without the enjoyment,—to convince myself that I have a property in the gay part of all the gilt chariots that I meet, which I regard as amusements designed to delight my eyes, and the imagination of those kind people who sit in them gayly attired only to please me." And so he goes on with a wonderful sense of pleasure and contentment, without the least feeling of envy, and without allowing the slightest room for it to exist. How grandly he does his casting of the account between real and imaginary pleasures. "But the pleasure which naturally affects a human mind with the most lively and transporting touches, I take to be the sense that we act in the eye of infinite wisdom, power, and goodness that will crown our virtuous endeavors here, with a happiness hereafter, large as our desires, and lasting as our immortal souls. This is a perpetual spring of gladness in the mind. This lessens our calamities, and doubles our joys. Without this, the highest state of life is insipid, and with it the lowest is a paradise." When a road leads to such a grand conclusion, you are pretty safe in travelling along it. It is along this one we desire you to go in your search for the pleasing refinement, that is to make you a pleasing companion on the way of life, and in those little gatherings by the wayside, which we denominate social. Along this road are the wayside flowers we desire you to pluck, and over its May-laden hedges are to be seen those beautiful pictures, which we desire you to cover the walls of your memory with. You will thrill and bound with the impulse of gladness, or be socially companionable with the quiet serenity of pleasant contentment. You will be sure to attain the minor purpose we have more immediately in view—you will begin in the spirit of not offending, and, as you gradually gain power, you will continue to gain favor for yourself, until your companionship is sought after for the profit and pleasure it imparts.

There are various little matters of tact and taste which are only to be acquired by the observation of example and the teaching of experience, but the great faculty and the disposition lie in such pursuits and associations. The elements of the conduct of life must be learned in some school wherein the actual conduct is but comparatively practical—where it is in a great measure merely ideal; and so the elements of good taste and the ideal of good breeding must be derived from the teachings of those eloquent instructors that catch the living manners as they rise, test them by the ideal of what is correct and becoming, and impress them on our minds with a quietness and a beauty, that make them pleasing for the time, and leave a happiness behind them for ever. So intimately knit in themselves and their consequences are the true, the good and the beautiful.

General Society.

To cultivate the art of pleasing is not only worthy of our ambition, but it is the dictate of humanity to render ourselves as agreeable as possible to those around us. While, therefore, we condemn that false system of philosophy which recommends the practice of flattery and deception for the purpose of winning the regard of those with whom we come in contact, we would rather urge the sincere and open conduct which is founded on moral principle, and which looks to the happiness of others, not through any sordid and selfish aim, but for the reward which virtuous actions bestow. Indeed, we do not discover the necessity of duplicity and hypocrisy in our intercourse with society. The virtues and the graces are not antagonistic. The sacrifice of personal convenience for the accommodation of others; the repression of our egotism and self-esteem; the occasional endurance of whatever is disagreeable or irksome to us through consideration for the infirmities of others, are not only some of the characteristics of true politeness, but are in the very spirit of benevolence, and, we might add, religion.

The English have a rule of etiquette, that if you are introduced to a person of higher position in society than yourself, you must never recognize him when you meet, until you see whether he intends to notice you. The meaning of this rule is, that you should be polite to nobody until you see whether they mean to be polite to you, which is simply refusing politeness in the name of politeness itself. There is a story of an unfortunate clerk of the Treasury, who dined one day at the Beefsteak Club, where he sat next to a duke, who conversed freely with him at dinner. The next day, meeting the duke in the street, he saluted him. But his grace, drawing himself up, said: "May I know, sir, to whom I have the honor of speaking?" "Why, we dined together at the club yesterday—I am Mr. Timms, of the Treasury," was the reply. "Then," said the duke, turning on his heel, "Mr. Timms, of the Treasury, I wish you *a good morning*." Though this anecdote is related in the English books as an example of etiquette, it is undoubtedly true that Mr. Timms, of the Treasury, was the politest man of the two; for even if he had made a mistake in being a little familiar in his politeness, had the duke been really a polite man he would have made the best of it, by returning the salutation, instead of the brutal mortification which he heaped upon the clerk of the Treasury. Everybody has read the anecdote of Washington, who politely returned the salutation of a negro, which caused his friend to ask if he "bowed to a negro." "To be sure

I do; do you think that I would allow a negro to outdo me in politeness?' said Washington. This is the American rule. Everybody in this
country may be polite to everybody—and if any one is too haughty and
too ill-bred to return the salutation, with him alone rests the responsibility and the shame.

A lady in company should never exhibit any anxiety to sing or play;
but if she intends to do so, she should not affect to refuse when asked,
but obligingly accede at once. If you cannot sing, or do not choose to,
say so with seriousness and gravity, and put an end to the expectation
promptly. After singing once or twice, cease and give place to others.
There is an old saying, that a singer can with the greatest difficulty be
set agoing, and when agoing, cannot be stopped.

Never commend a lady's musical skill to another lady who herself
plays.

Modern Chesterfields, who pretend to be superlatively well-bred, tell
one never to be "in a hurry." "To be in a hurry," say they, "is ill-
bred." The *dictum* is absurd. It is sometimes necessary to be hurried.
In the streets of the city one must hasten with the multitude. To walk
or lounge, as people who have nothing else to do, in Wall Street, or
Broadway, would be out of place and absurd. Judgment requires us,
not less than manners, to conform slightly with the behavior of those
with whom we associate or are forced to remain.

Never lose your temper at cards, and particularly avoid the exhibition
of anxiety or vexation at want of success. If you are playing whist, not
only keep your temper, but hold your tongue; any intimation to your
partner is decidedly ungentlemanly.

Do not take upon yourself to do the honors in another man's house,
nor constitute yourself master of the ceremonies, as you will thereby
offend the host and hostess.

Do not press before a lady at a theater or a concert. Always yield to
her, if practicable, your seat and place. Do not sit when she is standing, without offering her your place. Consult not only your own ease,
but also the comfort of those around you.

Do not cross a room in an anxious manner, and force your way up to
a lady merely to receive a bow, as by so doing you attract the eyes of the
company toward her. If you are desirous of being noticed by any one
in particular, put yourself in their way as if by accident, and do not let
them *see* that you have sought them out; unless, indeed, there be something very important to communicate.

Gentlemen who attend ladies to the opera, to concerts, to lectures,
etc., should take off their hats on entering the room, and while showing
them their seats. Having taken your seats remain quietly in them, and
avoid, unless absolute necessity requires it, incommoding others by
crowding out and in before them. If obliged to do this, politely apologize for the trouble you cause them. To talk during the performance
is an act of rudeness and injustice. You thus proclaim your own ill-
breeding and invade the rights of others, who have paid for the privilege
of hearing the performers, and not for listening to you.

If you are in attendance upon a lady at any opera, concert, or lecture, you should retain your seat at her side; but if you have no lady with you, and have taken a desirable seat, you should, if need be, cheerfully relinquish it in favor of a lady, for one less eligible.

To the opera, or theatre, ladies should wear opera hoods which are to be taken off on entering. In this country, custom permits the wearing of bonnets; but as they are neither convenient nor comfortable, ladies should dispense with their use whenever they can.

Gloves should be worn by ladies in church, and in places of public amusement. Do not take them off to shake hands. Great care should be taken that they are well made and fit neatly.

If you would have your children grow up beloved and respected by their elders as well as their contemporaries, teach them good manners in their childhood. The young sovereign should first learn to obey, that he may be the better fitted to command in his turn.

Show, but do not show off, your children to strangers. Recollect, in the matter of children, how many are born every hour, each one almost as remarkable as yours in the eyes of its papa and mamma.

Notwithstanding that good general breeding is easy of attainment, and is, in fact, attained by most people, yet we may enlarge upon a saying of Emerson's, by declaring that the world has never yet seen "a perfect gentleman."

It is not deemed polite and respectful to smoke in the presence of ladies, even though they are amiable enough to permit it. A gentleman, therefore, is not in the habit of smoking in the parlor, for if there is nobody present to object, it leaves a smell in the room which the wife has good reason to be mortified at, if discovered by her guests.

It is very common to see persons eat, drink, and smoke to excess. Such habits are vulgar in the lowest degree. Some men pride themselves on their abilities in drinking and smoking—more especially in the latter. These are blunders that need no reasoning to expose them. The man who exhibits a tendency to excesses will, sooner or later, be shunned by all except a few of his own stamp, and not even by them be respected. Guard against excess in all things, as neither gentlemanly nor human.

Spitting is a filthy habit, and annoys one in almost every quarter, indoors and out. Since vulgarity has had its way so extensively amongst us, every youth begins to smoke and spit before he has well cut his teeth. Smoking is unquestionably so great a pleasure to those accustomed to it, that it must not be condemned, yet the spitting associated with it detracts very much from the enjoyment. No refined person will spit where ladies are present, or in any public promenade; the habit is digusting in the extreme, and one would almost wish that it could be checked in public by means of law.

Never scratch your head, pick you teeth, clean your nails, or, worse than all, pick your nose in company; all these things are disgusting.

To indulge in ridicule, whether the subject be present or absent, is to descend below the level of gentlemanly propriety. Your skill may excite laughter, but will not insure respect.

A reverential regard for religious observances, and religious opinions, is a distinguishing trait of a refined mind. Whatever your opinions on the subject, you are not to intrude them on others, perhaps to the shaking of their faith and happiness. Religious topics should be avoided in conversation, except where all are prepared to concur in a respectful treatment of the subject. In mixed societies the subject should never be introduced.

Frequent consultation of the watch or time-pieces is impolite, either when at home or abroad. If at home, it appears as if you were tired of your company and wished them to be gone; if abroad, as if the hours dragged heavily, and you were calculating how soon you would be released.

Never read in company. A gentleman or lady may, however, look over a book of engravings with propriety.

The simpler, and the more easy and unconstrained your manners, the more you will impress people of your good breeding. *Affectation* is one of the brazen marks of vulgarity.

It is very unbecoming to exhibit petulance, or angry feeling, though it is indulged in so largely in almost every circle. The true gentleman does not suffer his countenance to be easily ruffled; and we only look paltry when we suffer temper to hurry us into ill-judged expressions of feeling. "He that is soon angry dealeth foolishly."

Commands should never be given in a commanding tone. A gentleman requests, he does not command. We are not to assume so much importance, whatever our station, as to give orders in the "imperative mood," nor are we ever justified in thrusting the consciousness of servitude on any one. The blunder of commanding sternly is most frequently committed by those who have themselves but just escaped servitude, and we should not exhibit to others a weakness so unbecoming.

It is a great thing to be able to *walk like a gentleman*—that is, to get rid of the awkward, lounging, swinging gait of a clown, and stop before you reach the affected and flippant step of a dandy. In short, nothing but *being a gentleman* can ever give you the air and step of one. A man who has a shallow or an impudent brain will be quite sure to show it in his heels, in spite of all that rules of manners can do for him.

A gentleman never sits in the house with his hat on in the presence of ladies for a single moment. Indeed, so strong is the force of habit, that a gentleman will quite unconsciously remove his hat on entering a parlor, or drawing-room, even if there is no one present but himself. People who sit in the house with their hats on are to be suspected of having spent the most of their time in bar-roooms, and similar places. *A gentleman never sits with his hat on in the theatre.* Gentlemen do not generally sit even in an eating-room with their hats on, if there is any convenient place to put them.

The books on etiquette will tell you, that on waiting on a lady into a carriage, or the box of a theatre, you are to take off your hat; but such *is not* the custom among polite people in this country. The inconvenience of such a rule is a good reason against its observance in a country where the practice of politeness has in it nothing of the servility which

is often attached to it in countries where the code of etiquette is dictated
by the courts of monarchy. In handing a lady into a carriage, a gentleman *may* need to employ both his hands, and he has no third hand to
hold on to his hat.

Cleanliness of person is a distinguishing trait of every well-bred person; and this not on state occasions only, dut at all times, even at home.
It is a folly to sit by the fire in a slovenly state, consoling oneself with
the remark, "Nobody will call to-day." Should somebody call we
are in no plight to receive them, and otherwise it is an injury to the character to allow slovenly habits to control us even when we are unseen.

Chesterfield inveighs against holding a man by the button, "for if people are not willing to hear you, you had much better hold your tongue
than them." Button-holing is not a common vice, but pointing, nudg-
ing, hitting a man in the side with your fist, or giving him a kick of recognition under the table, are too common not to be noticed here as terrible breaches of deportment. Significant looks and gestures are equally
objectionable, and must be avoided by all who desire to soar above positive vulgarity. I have often been annoyed by hearing a friend discourse
on some person's failings or excellences, the person referred to being only
known to the speaker. It is a bad rule to talk of persons at all, but more
especially if the person spoken of is not known to all the listeners.

Do not offer a person the chair from which you have just risen, unless
there be no other in the room.

Never take the chair usually occupied by the lady or gentleman of the
house, even though they be absent, nor use the snuff-box of another,
unless he offer it.

Do not lean your head against the wall. You will either soil the paper,
or get your hair well powdered with lime

Do not touch any of the ornaments in the houses where you visit; they
are meant only for the use of the lady of the house, and may be admired,
but not touched.

Lord Chesterfield, in his "Advice to his Son," justly characterizes an
absent man as unfit for business or conversation. Absence of mind is
usually affected, and springs in most cases from a desire to be thought
abstracted in profound contemplations. The world, however, gives a
man no credit for vast ideas who exhibits absence when he should be attentive, even to trifles. The world is right in this, and I would implore
every studious youth to forget that he is studious when he enters company. I have seen many a man, who would have made a bright character otherwise, affect a foolish reserve, remove himself as far from others
as possible, and in mixed assembly, where social prattle or sincere conversation enlivened the hearts of the company, sit by himself abstracted
in a book. It is foolish, and, what is worse for the absentee, it looks so.
A hint on this subject is sufficient, and we do hint, that abstractedness
of manner should never be exhibited; the geniuses have ever been attentive to trifles when it so behooved them.

Affectation of superiority galls the feelings of those to whom it is offered. In company with an inferior, never let him feel his inferiority. An
employer, who invites his confidential clerk to his house, should treat

him in every way the same as his most distinguished guest. No reference to business should be made, and anything in the shape of command avoided. It is very easy by a look, a word, the mode of reception, or otherwise, to advertise to the other guests, "This is my clerk," or, "The person I now treat as a guest was yesterday laboring in my service;" but such a thing would lower the host more than it would annoy the guests. Before Burns had arrived at his high popularity, he was once invited by some puffed-up lairds to dine, in order that they might have the gratification of hearing the poet sing one of his own songs. Burns was shown into the servants' hall, and left to dine with the menials. After dinner he was invited to the drawing-room, and a glass of wine being handed to him, requested to sing one of his own songs. He immediately gave his entertainers that thrilling assertion of independence, "A man's a man for a' that," and left the moment he had finished, his heart embittered at patronage offered in a manner so insulting to his poverty.

People who have risen in the world are too apt to suppose they render themselves of consequence *in proportion to the pride they display*, and their want of attention toward those with whom they come in contact. This is a terrible mistake, as every ill-bred act recoils with triple violence against its perpetrators, leading the offended parties to analyze them, and to question the right of assuming a superiority to which they are but rarely entitled.

Punctuality is one of the characteristics of politeness. He who does not keep his appointments promptly is unfit for the society of gentlemen, and will soon find himself shut out from it.

In private, watch your thoughts; in your family, watch your temper; in society, watch your tongue.

Avoid restlessness in company, lest you make the whole party as fidgety as yourself. "Do not beat the 'Devil's tattoo' by drumming with your fingers on the table; it cannot fail to annoy every one within hearing, and is the index of a vacant mind. Neither read the newspaper in an audible whisper, as it disturbs the attention of those near you. Both these bad habits are particularly offensive where most common, that is, in a counting or news-room. Remember, that a carelessness as to what may incommode others is the sure sign of a coarse and ordinary mind; indeed, the essential part of good breeding is more in the avoidance of whatever may be disagreeable to others, than even an accurate observance of the customs of good society."

Good sense must, in many cases, determine good breeding; because the same thing that would be civil at one time and to one person, may be quite otherwise at another time and to another person.

Chesterfield says, "As learning, honor, and virtue are absolutely necessary to gain you the esteem and admiration of mankind, politeness and good breeding are equally necessary to make you welcome and agreeable in conversation and common life. Great talents, such as honor, virtue, learning, and parts, are above the generality of the world, who neither possess them themselves nor judge of them rightly in others; but all people are judges of the lesser talents, such as civility, affability, and an obliging, agreeable address and manner; because they feel the good effects of them, as making society easy and pleasing."

If you are in a public room, as a library or reading-room, avoid loud conversation or laughing, which may disturb others.   At the opera, or a concert, be profoundly silent during the performances; if you do not wish to hear the music, you have no right to interfere with the enjoyment of others.

In accompanying ladies to any public place, as to a concert or lecture, you should precede them in entering the room, and procure seats for them.

Never allow a lady to get a chair for herself, ring a bell, pick up a handkerchief or glove she may have dropped, or, in short, perform any service for herself which you can perform for her, when you are in the room.   By extending such courtesies to your mother, sister, or other members of your family, they become habitual, and are thus more grace-fully performed when abroad.

Etiquette in church is entirely out of place; but we may here observe that a conversation wantonly profligate always offends against good man-ners, nor can an irreligious man ever achieve that bearing which consti-tutes the true gentleman.   He may be very polished and observant of forms, and even if so, he will, out of respect for others, refrain from in-truding his opinoins and abstain from attacking those of others.

Chesterfield says, "Civility is particularly due to all women; and, re-member, that no provocation whatsoever can justify any man in not being civil to every woman; and the greatest man would justly be reckoned a brute if he were not civil to the meanest woman.   It is due to their sex, and is the only protection they have against the superior strength of ours; nay, even a little is allowable with women; and a man may, without weakness, tell a woman she is either handsomer or wiser than she is."

Keep your engagements.   Nothing is ruder than to make engagement, be it of business or pleasure, and break it.   If your memory is not suffi-ciently retentive to keep all the engagements you make stored within it, carry a little memorandum book and enter them there.   Especially keep any appointment made with a lady, for, depend upon it, the fair sex for-give any other fault in good breeding sooner than a broken engagement.

The right of privacy is sacred, and should always be respected.   It is exceedingly improper to enter a private room anywhere without knock-ing.   No relation, however intimate, will justify an abrupt intrusion upon a private apartment.   So the trunks, boxes, packets, papers, and letters of every individual, locked or unlocked, sealed or unsealed, are sacred. It is ill-manners even to open a book-case, or to read a written paper lying open, without permission expressed or implied.   Books in an open case or on a center-table, cards in a card-case, and newspapers, are pre-sumed to be open for examination.   Be careful where you go, what you read, and what you handle, particularly in private apartments.

Avoid intermeddling with the affairs of others.   This is a most com-mon fault.   A number of people seldom meet but they begin discussing the affairs of some one who is absent.   This is not only uncharitable but positively unjust.   It is equivalent to trying a *cause in the absence of the person implicated*.   Even in the criminal code a prisoner is presumed to be innocent until he is found guilty.   Society, however, is less just, and passes judgment without hearing the defence.   Depend upon it, as a certain rule, *that the people who unite with you in discussing the affairs of others will proceed to scandalize you the moment that you depart.*

Be well read also, for the sake of the general company and the ladies' in the literature of the day. You will thereby enlarge the regions of pleasurable talk. Besides, it is often necessary. Haslitt, who had entertained an unfounded prejudice against Dickens's works when they were first written, confesses that he was at last obliged to read them, because he could not enter a mixed company without hearing them admired and quoted.

Always conform your conduct, as near as possible, to the company with whom you are associated. If you should be thrown among people who are vulgar, it is better to humor them than to set yourself up, then and there, for a model of politeness. It is related of a certain king that on a particular occasion he turned his tea into his saucer, contrary to the etiquette of society, because two country ladies, whose hospitalities he was enjoying, did so. That king was a gentleman; and this anecdote serves to illustrate an important principle: namely, that true politeness and genuine good manners often not only permit, but absolutely demand, a violation of some of the arbitrary rules of etiquette. Bear this fact in mind.

Miscellaneous

A gentleman or lady will never look over the shoulder of another who is either reading or writing.

No gentleman or lady will ever be guilty of personality in conversation.

Exaggeration trespasses so closely upon falsehood that it is not safe to trust it. A strict adherence to truth never leads to error.

Conceit is the vice or folly of the shallow minded. The truly wise man is modest, and the braggart and coxcomb are valued but little.

It is unladylike to stand with arms akimbo or folded.

It is a mark of low breeding to fidget either with the hands or feet; to play with the watch chain, toss the gloves, suck the head of a cane or handle of a parasol, or to fuss with a collar or necktie. Quiet ease is a certain sign of gentle breeding.

To swing the foot or tap monotonously with the feet, to drum with the fingers on a table or window, are all breaches of etiquette.

Never speak of persons with whom you are but slightly acquainted by their first name.

No true lady will ever allow herself to speak of a gentleman by his surname without a prefix.

No gentleman will ever criticize a wine offered to him, no matter how poor it may be.

Flattery is a breach of etiquette.

No gentleman may ever break an engagement, whether it be one of business or pleasure, with a lady or with another gentleman.

Irritability is a breach of good manners.

Observe strict punctuality. It is a positive unkindness to keep another waiting.

Never pare or scrape your nails, pick your teeth, comb your hair, or perform any of the necessary operations of the toilet in company.

Never answer a civil question rudely, or even impatiently.

No gentleman may ever refuse an apology.

Never intrude upon a business man during business hours.

It is an act of impertinence to question a child or a servant upon family affairs.

It is a breach of etiquette to consult your watch when in company

Never assume a lazy, lounging attitude when in company.

Mysterious allusions are rude.

Never rise to take leave in the midst of an interesting conversation.

A gentleman will never talk of his business affairs to a lady, nor a lady weary her gentleman friends by an account of her domestic affairs.

The only gifts that may be offered or accepted between ladies and gentlemen who are not related or engaged are books, flowers, music, or confectionery. A lady who accepts costly presents of jewelry puts herself under an obligation that she may find troublesome, and no true gentleman will expose a lady to the pain of refusing an improper gift of this kind.

Before taking a place at table, say "good morning ," or "good evening," to those in the room before you, and especially to those who preside over the meal.

Never go into company with the breath tainted by eating onions, garlic, cheese, or any other strong scented food.

It is a breach of etiquette for a gentleman to enter a lady's presence smelling of tobacco or wine.

It is a breach of etiquette to send a present hoping for another.

Also to refer to a gift you have made, a favor you have granted, or an obligation of any kind under which another lies with regard to you. Husband or wife should not speak of each other by their initial. Do not say "D. gave me this," or I refer such matters to Mrs. H." It is a mark of ill breeding.

Do not be too familiar towards a new acquaintance. It sometimes proves offensive.

It is not only a breach of etiquette of the grossest kind, but evidences want of humanity and good feeling as well, to notice, by look or words, any deformity, any scar or misfortune to the face or figure of a friend.

When offering a gift, do not represent it as valueless or useless to yourself.

It is often said that fools only laugh at their own wit. Don't do it.

Never write your own remarks in a borrowed book.

Do not scold. It is ill-bred.

None but a boor will insult his inferiors.

Do not display bashfulness in society. Avoid vice and ignorance, and you may go anywhere without fear or concern.

Never wear an air of abstraction in society. It is more frequently a proof of self conceit than of genius.

Eccentricity of any kind is in bad taste.

Many persons, from a real or fancied personal resemblance to some celebrity, will ape their manners also, as if mere appearance would make them equally distinguished. It is great folly.

If you meet with reverses, it is wiser to withdraw from society than to have society withdraw from you.

It is a gross breach of etiquette to contradict any one.

He who would suffer himself to speak a word against a woman, or to rail at women generally, is unworthy of the name of man, unworthy of the mother who bore him, and should be relegated to obscurity.

Do not try to make yourself appear more important than you really are. You run the risk of being considered less so.

Egotism adorns no one. "I, me, and mine" should be bowed out of genteel society.

Chesterfield says; "The scholar, without good breeding, is a pedant; the philosopher, a cynic; the soldier, a brute; and every one disagreeable."

In private, watch your thoughts; in your family, watch your temper; in society, watch your tongue.

If you cannot keep good company, keep none. It is better to live alone than in low company.

Avoid entering a room noisely, slamming the door, or stamping heavily upon the floor.

It is a breach of etiquette to neglect calling upon your friend. Visiting forms the chord which binds society together, and it is so firmly tied that were the knot severed, society would perish.

Do not answer a serious remark by a flippant one.

Practical joking cannot be too highly censured.

Never pass between two persons who are conversing together.

If you are necessitated to pass *before* anybody, it must be done with an apology.

Do not urge wine upon a guest who has already declined to drink.

Do not call a new acquaintance by the Christian name, unless requested to do so.

If you write requesting an autograph, always enclose a postage stamp for the reply.

Ladies should avoid the use of strong perfumes. They are unpleasant to nauseating to some persons; and it is a breach of etiquette to annoy other people.

A lady should not wear at home faded or spotted gowns, or soiled finery, or anything that is not neat and appropriate. Appear at the

4

breakfast table in some perfectly pure and delicate attire—fresh, cool, and delicious, like a newly plucked flower. Dress for the pleasure and admiration of your family.

Avoid servile submission to fashion. Believe in your own instincts and the mirror rather than the *dicta* of the mantua makers, and modify modes to suit your personal peculiarities. At the period in which this is written our streets are peopled with both males and females bedecked in all the colors of the rainbow, all of which is too *blazé* for true gentility. Quiet modes are much better, and "set off" the wearer to finer effect.

Always acknowledge by note all invitations, whether accepted or not. Never leave a letter unanswered. Acknowledge all courtesies, all attentions, all kindnesses.

When in company, do not dwell on the beauty of women not present; on the splendor of other people's houses; on the success of other people's entertainments; in the superiority of anybody. Excessive praise of people or things elsewhere implies discontent with people or things present.

There are some who practically adopt the opinion that the courteous observances of social and domestic life are wholly inapplicable to business intercourse. This is wrong. Good breeding is not a thing to be put off and on with varying outward circumstances. If genuine, it will always exhibit itself as certainly as integrity. The manifestations of this will vary with occasion; but it will nevertheless be apparent at all times and to all observers when its legitimate influence is rightly understood and admitted. Though the observance of elaborate ceremony in the more practical associations of busy outer life would be absurdly inappropriate, that careful respect for the rights and feelings of others, which is the basis of all true politeness, should not under these circumstances be disregarded.

The secret of the superior popularity of some business men with their compeers and employees lies often rather in any other characteristic. You may observe in one instance a universal favorite, to whom all his associates extend a welcoming hand as though there were magic in the ready smile and genial manner, and who is served by his inferiors in station with cheerfulness and alacrity, indicating that a little more than a business bond draws them to him; and again, an upright but externally repulsive man, though always commanding respect from his compeers, holds them aloof by his frigidity, and receives the service of fear rather than of love from those to whom he may be always just and even humane, if never sympathizing and unbending.

And finally, to sum up all, we would remind you that a dignified and pleasing manner can only fit truthfully and gracefully a worthy and manly nature; that the ease and dignity of the true man or woman can only flow from native worth; and that a faithful observance of the rules and principles herein set forth will enable you to avoid any glaring impropriety, and do much to render you easy and confident in society.

Popular Books.—Sent post-paid at the Prices Marked

De Witt's Little Gems in Prose and Verse for
LITTLE PEOPLE. A careful compilation of choice little pieces, suitable
for reading and recitation by the smallest readers and speakers. Sent
by mail, post-paid, on receipt of **10 Cents.**

Wehman's Little Dialogues for Little People. A
charming and entirely new collection of original prose and verse dialogues, written expressly for the purpose of providing short, bright
pieces which can be easily memorized by small children. Sent by mail,
post-paid, on receipt of **10 Cents.**

Wehman's Little Folks' Verses. Containing an un-
equalled collection of choice verses suitable for recitations for little folks.
Youthful readers cannot fail to find some verses to suit their peculiar
genius in this book. There isn't a dull line in this book—everything crisp
and crackling. Sent by mail, postpaid, on receipt of **10 Cents.**

Wehman's Home Songs for Little People. Con-
taining a fine collection of jingling rhymes, adapted both in thought and
language for recitation by the very youngest speakers. Its articles are
full of meaning, and will tend to instill many "good things" in their
youthful minds. Sent by mail, post-paid, on receipt of **10 Cents.**

Wehman's Rhymes and Jingles for Little Speak-
ERS. As the title suggests, so the contents of this book. All the selections are short and bright, and easily memorized, and comprise many of
the most charming verses ever written for children. Sent by mail, post-
paid, on receipt of **10 Cents.** U. S. postage stamps taken same as cash.

De Witt's Wee Pieces and Dialogues for Our
DARLINGS. It is seldom that nice little dialogues can be found without
searching the pages of a great many books; but here is a fine lot of them,
joined to other very pretty pieces. They are just the things for children
to learn when they first begin to speak at school, or in the parlor. Sent
by mail, post-paid, on receipt of **10 Cents.**

De Witt's Little Speeches for Little Folks. Being
a careful compilation of many of the prettiest small pieces ever written
for the use of our little ones just stepping from babyhood to childhood.
A book exactly fitted to amuse and interest the very smallest young
lispers; such as have just begun to speak and understand plain words
and sentences. Sent by mail, post-paid, on receipt of **10 Cents.**

Wehman's Children's Dialogues. This book contains
a fine collection of short, easy dialogues, carefully prepared, and suitable for children from four to eight years of age. Many of these dialogues have been written expressly for this book and cannot be found
elsewhere. It is a book that any wise mother can safely place in the
hands of her darlings. Sent by mail, post-paid, on receipt of **10 Cents.**

Wehman's Children's Speaker. A careful compila-
tion of short pieces suitable for recitation by children from four to eight
years of age, including well selected pieces for special and holiday occasions. This book will please every parent, as it contains a good variety
of interesting and instructive pieces for children. Sent by mail, post-
paid, on receipt of **10 Cents.** U. S. postage stamps taken same as cash.

ADDRESS ALL ORDERS TO

HENRY J. WEHMAN, Publisher, 108 Park Row, New York.

Popular Books.—Sent post-paid at the Prices Marked

De Witt's Choice Readings and Select Recitations,
No. 1. This book, the first of the series, contains 40 choice readings and recitations upon a variety of subjects, and all interesting. In short, quantity, quality, and low price are its salient features. Sent by mail, post-paid, on receipt of **10 Cents.**

Macaulay's Acting Dialogues.
Containing nearly one hundred of the finest dialogues in the language, including choice pieces for from two to fifteen characters. These pieces are all eminently dramatic, affording every speaker a good chance to ACT OUT the different parts. Sent by mail, post-paid, on receipt of **25 Cents.**

De Witt's Choice Readings and Select Recitations,
No. 2. This book, the second of the series, contains 48 choice readings and recitations upon a variety of subjects, and all interesting. The contents of this book is entirely different from No. 1. In short, quantity, quality, and low price are its salient features. Sent by mail, post-paid, on receipt of **10 Cents.** U. S. postage stamps taken same as cash.

De Witt's Choice Readings and Select Recitations,
No. 3. This book, the third of the series, contains 60 choice readings and recitations upon a variety of subjects, and all interesting. The contents of this book is entirely different from Nos. 1 and 2. In short, quantity, quality and low price are its salient features. Sent by mail, post-paid, on receipt of **10 Cents.** Clean and unused U. S. postage stamps taken same as cash.

De Witt's Choice Readings and Select Recitations,
No. 4. This book, the fourth of the series, contains 58 choice readings and recitations upon a variety of subjects, and all interesting. The contents of this book is entirely different from Nos. 1, 2 and 3. In short, quantity, quality, and low price are its salient features. Sent by mail, post-paid, on receipt of **10 Cents.** Clean and unused United States postage stamps taken same as cash.

De Witt's Choice Readings and Select Recitations,
No. 5. This book, the fifth of the series, contains 44 choice readings and recitations upon a variety of subjects, and all interesting. The contents of this book is entirely different from Nos. 1, 2, 3 and 4. In short, quantity, quality, and low price are its salient features. Sent by mail, post-paid, on receipt **10 Cents.** Clean and unused United States postage stamps taken same as cash.

Gus Williams' Standard Recitations.
Containing a great number of pathetic, powerful, instructive and humorous articles by the best authors of the times, many of which have been delivered by the compiler, with every mark of popular appreciation, before large and intellectual audiences throughout the United States. Printed on a good quality of paper, from clear, readable type, and bound substantially in handsome paper cover. Sent by mail, post-paid, on receipt of **10 Cents.**

Wehman's Selection of Popular Dialogues, No. 1.
This book, the first of the series, contains a large number of the finest dialogues in our language. Adapted for parlor entertainments, social gatherings, school exhibitions, etc. Many of the dialogues in this book are new and original and cannot be found in any other book. Great care has been taken in the preparation of this work, our chief aim being to insert nothing but the "cream" of the "whole field" of popular dialogues, suitable for private or public recital. Sent by mail, post-paid, on receipt of **25 Cents.** U. S. postage stamps taken same as cash.

ADDRESS ALL ORDERS TO

HENRY J. WEHMAN, Publisher, 108 Park Row, New York

Popular Books.—Sent post-paid at the Prices Marked

De Witt's Challenge School Speaker. A choice collection of stirring, effective, and brilliant gems, expressly prepared for the display of forensic talent, whether tragic, pathetic, or argumentative. Sent by mail, post-paid, on receipt of **10 Cents.**

De Witt's Improved School Speaker. This book is in every way an improvement on nine-tenths of the Speakers published. All the pieces are of a kind that must make them heartily liked by both teachers and pupils. There is not a heavy, dull article in the work. Sent by mail, post-paid, on receipt of **10 Cents.**

De Witt's Perfection School Speaker. No other collection of pieces has any right to be compared to this. It is the very best of them. There isn't a chip of dead wood in it. Every speech is marked by some excellent quality, either of subject or expression. Sent by mail, post-paid, on receipt of **10 Cents.**

De Witt's Irish Dialect School Speaker. A carefully compiled collection of Irish dialect pieces in prose and poetry, some of which are pathetic, some dramatic and soul-stirring, and others full of irresistible Irish humor. Suitable for school, parlor or platform recital. Sent by mail, post-paid, on receipt of **10 Cents.**

De Witt's Patriotic School Speaker. Filled with the noblest bursts of patriotic eloquence, in prose and verse. Every youth that feels—as all should feel—that he has a country to admire and love, should master the brilliant specimens of oratory that abound in this book. Sent by mail, post-paid, on receipt of **10 Cents.**

De Witt's Temperance School Speaker. A fine collection of recitations and readings suitable for schools, temperance meetings, anniversaries, and social gatherings. Much of its contents will tend to make an indelible impression upon youthful minds as to the evil effects of intemperance. Price, by mail, post-paid, **10 Cents.**

De Witt's Primary School Speaker. Containing a variety of pieces adapted both in thought and language for recitation by the very youngest speakers. In many "Speakers" intended for young children, the authors get together a number of pieces only noticeable for jingling rhymes; in this book all the articles are full of meaning, without being dull or prosy. Sent by mail, post-paid, on receipt of **10c.**

De Witt's Dramatic School Speaker. Containing a large number of the most effective, eloquent, instructive, and brilliant pieces for public and private schools and academies. Many of the articles in this book are the most admired specimens in our language, expressive of every shade of feeling and passion. Every youthful reader can find some pieces to suit his peculiar genius in this book. Sent by mail, post-paid, on receipt of **10 Cents.**

De Witt's Comic School Speaker. Containing an unequalled collection of the most amusing, eccentric, droll, and humorous pieces, suitable for recitation in schools or at drawing-room entertainments. It would be impossible to find so many irresistibly funny pieces in any other tongue. They range from the most refined wit to the broadest farcical humor; but always free from even an approach to vulgarity. Sent by mail, post-paid, on receipt of **10 Cents.**

ADDRESS ALL ORDERS TO

HENRY J. WEHMAN, Publisher, 108 Park Row, New York

Popular Books.—Sent post-paid at the Prices Marked

Wehman's Book on Skating. Full instructions for plain and fancy skating, and all games and sports on the ice. Sent by mail, post-paid, on receipt of 10 Cents.

Wehman's Gymnastic Exercises. For the development of the muscles and stature. Bar and trapeze exercises, vaulting, climbing, lifting, etc. Sent by mail, post-paid, on receipt of 10 Cents.

Wehman's Field Sports for Boys. Rules and regulations for the popular English games of hare and hounds, prisoner's base, hockey, leap-frog, trap, etc. Sent by mail, post-paid, on receipt of 10 Cents. U. S. postage stamps taken same as cash.

Wehman's Football. Practical instructions on the duties of players and their positions; rules of the game as played by prominent clubs and associations; instructions for umpiring, etc. Sent by mail, post-paid, on receipt of 10 Cents.

Wehman's Athletic Exercises for Health and STRENGTH. Giving full directions for training, walking, running, leaping, using dumb-bells (both English and French method), Indian clubs, etc. Sent by mail, post-paid, on receipt of 10 Cents.

Wehman's Athletic Games of Skill. Giving full instructions for the games of bowling, racquet and fives, skittles (both Dutch and French), the Scotch game of golf, etc. Also, athletic feats with the sword. Sent by mail, post-paid, on receipt of 10 Cents.

Wehman's Wizards' Manual. The greatest book ever issued of its kind. Complete compendium of the secrets of the Magician, Mind Reader and Ventriloquist. Every detail carefully explained and fully illustrated. It explains—How to Change Paper and Bran to Milk and Sugar, How to Cut a Lady in Halves, and hundreds of other marvelous feats of legerdemain. It also teaches how to read a person's thoughts, so that you can reveal numbers and names thought of, find hidden articles, etc. Sent by mail, post-paid, on receipt of 25 Cents.

Wehman's New Book of Tricks and Ventriloquists' GUIDE. The latest and best book published on tricks, ventriloquism, second sight and fireside mesmerism. Illustrated with nearly 100 engravings. The instructions are so plainly given that any one, with a little practice, can do the tricks, as they only require SIMPLE APPARATUS. A few of the tricks are: How to eat a peck of shavings and change them to ribbon; how to make a dime pass through a table; how to make fire burn under water; how to cut off a chicken's head without killing it, etc. Sent by mail, post-paid, on receipt of 25 Cents.

Maccabe's Art of Ventriloquism and Vocal Illu- SIONS, with full directions to learners; showing how to practice ventriloquism; with amusing dialogues for beginners, including the "Repertoire" of the English railway porter, as performed by Frederick Maccabe in his celebrated ventriloquial entertainments. Beginning with the rudiments, this book shows the use of a mirror; the proper position of the lips; how to give the idea of "distance" to sounds; the use of the "falsetto" and the "guttural"; imitations of different animals, amusing experiments, ventriloquial dialogues, etc. Together with valuable hints in regard to breathing, speaking and singing. Sent by mail, post-paid, on receipt of 10 Cents. U. S. postage stamps taken same as cash.

ADDRESS ALL ORDERS TO

HENRY J. WEHMAN, Publisher, 108 Park Row, New York

Popular Books—Sent Post-Paid at the Prices Marked

De Witt's Columbian School Speaker. A choice collection of recitations especially arranged and adapted for patriotic celebrations, such as Fourth of July, Decoration Day, and Grand Army Reunions. These pieces will serve to tincture youthful minds with true American, patriotic spirit, also to kindle the patriotism of American listeners. Sent by mail, post-paid, on receipt of **10 Cents.**

De Witt's Humorous School Speaker. Containing a choice selection of pieces in prose and verse that will "serve to make those laugh who never laughed before, and those who always laugh laugh all the more." Such pieces are always in demand. There isn't a dull or objectionable line in this book, and it is, therefore, a good book to place in the hands of young, humorously-inclined reciters. Sent by mail, post-paid, on receipt of **10 Cents.**

De Witt's Academic School Speaker. Containing a selection of pieces especially adapted to the school and academy. It contains pieces by the most celebrated authors, such as Charles Dickens, Robert Burns, Sir Walter Scott, Shakespeare, W. C. Bryant, Oliver Goldsmith, Lord Macaulay, John Milton, Lord Byron, Thomas Gray, Thomas Campbell, and many others. Sent by mail, post-paid, on receipt of **TEN CENTS.** U. S. postage stamps taken same as cash.

De Witt's Exhibition School Speaker. Comprising very many of the most exquisite pieces in our language, particularly adapted for recitation in public. There is no accomplishment that imparts such a nameless grace as the faculty of reading and reciting plainly and eloquently. This work furnishes many of the finest pieces for elocutionary effect in the language. Sent by mail, post-paid, on receipt of **10 Cents.** U. S. postage stamps taken same as cash.

De Witt's Thespian School Speaker. Containing pieces that have been recited on the stage and in the drawing-room by many of our leading actors and actresses. It contains 40 selections by well-known authors, such as Shakespeare, Tennyson, Clement Scott, Knowles, Lowell, Whittier, Swinburne, Bulwer, Southey, Brougham, Cornwall, Buchannan and many others. Its contents comprises some of the finest pieces in the English language. Price, by mail, post-paid, **TEN CENTS.** U. S. postage stamps taken same as cash.

De Witt's American School Speaker. Containing 63 choice selections for declamation and recitation, suitable for school, parlor or platform recital. The following are a few of its selections, viz.:—The American Indians—Character of Washington—Modern Republics—Evils of War—Liberty and Greatness—American Institutions—Christianity the Basis of Liberty—The Land of Our Birth—The Warrior—The Ship of State—The World—and 52 other first-class pieces. Big value at nominal cost. Sent by mail, post-paid, on receipt of **10 Cents.**

De Witt's Platform School Speaker. A collection of new recitations for parlor and school entertainment purposes. By Dora Y. Burtis. These selections are unhackneyed, many of them never before having appeared in print. An entire evening's entertainment can be taken from its pages without a padding of time-honored, but worn recitations; this merit, if no other, insures its success. Professional and amateur, teacher and student, will find in this book a combination of material valuable and interesting. Sent by mail, post-paid, on receipt of **10 Cents.** U. S. postage stamps taken same as cash.

ADDRESS ALL ORDERS TO

HENRY J. WEHMAN, Publisher, 108 Park Row, New York

Popular Books.—Sent post-paid at the Prices Marked

Gus Williams' World of Humor. A collection of humorous stories, queer anecdotes, Dutch and Irish drolleries, jolly jokes, and bright sayings. Compiled by that prince of humorists, Gus Williams. Sent by mail, post-paid, on receipt of **25 Cents.**

Pat Rooney's Quaint Conundrums and Funny GAGS. Interlarded with Irish wit and humor, Chinese sketches, humorous anecdotes, and mirth-provoking stories. A capital book for end men in minstrel entertainments. Sent by mail, post-paid, on receipt of **25c.** United States postage stamps taken same as cash.

Wehman's Budget of Jokes. This new budget of jokes has been "launched into existence" with a rich cargo of rib-tickling, side-splitting, button-bursting jokes and witticisms, embracing Irish bulls, Dutch comicalities, Yankee yarns, comical hits, flowers of wit, excruciating jokes, end men's gags, jolly jokes, ludicrous drolleries, sable witticisms, and many other kinds "that touch the funny bone" every time. Sent by mail, post-paid, on receipt of **25 Cents.**

Byron Christy's Black Clown Joke Book. Nothing is more popular and acceptable to an intelligent audience than negro wit and humor. In this book will be found some of the most funny things published in colored dialogue, witty sayings, mirth-provoking poems, etc. This should not be confounded with worthless imitations on the same subject, published and advertised largely by irresponsible concerns. There will be found in this work stories and jokes that appear in no other publication. Sent by mail, post-paid, on receipt of **10 Cents.**

Wehman's Budget of Irish Jokes. The wit of the Irish is world-renowned. In this book will be found fun for every Irishman, and all the rest of mankind; in fact, Fenian fun, Welshman's wit, and Corkonian comicalities. Other tribes not mentioned will laugh until green tears roll down their cheeks. The jokes in this book are new and are used by the most celebrated Irish comedians. This book embraces a collection of funny stories, jokes and conundrums, interspersed with witty sayings, grinning gags, and humorous dialogues, suitable for all occasions. Every joke in the book is as valuable to an Irish comedian as a nugget of gold to a miner. Read it and dispell the "blues." Recite the jokes in an empty room, and the portraits of friends and relatives, on the wall, will be noticed to grin. If you want hot, roasted, boiled and baked Irish jokes, fit to serve at all times, send for this fun producer. Sent by mail, post-paid, on receipt of **25 Cents.**

Wehman's Budget of Dutch Jokes. In this book, just published, will be found the latest side-splitting, button-bursting, hot-roasted, rip-roaring Dutch dialect jokes, comicalities and funny hits, such as used by the celebrated Dutch comedians, Weber & Fields, Sam Bernard, Gus Williams, and Geo. S. Knight. Every page is brim-full and over-flowing with the richest of Dutch wit of every description, both in prose and verse, which never fail to produce roars of laughter. This book will afford fun for a life-time, and we beg those persons who are affected with lung trouble not to buy it, as the laughter it produces on a reader may do them serious injury. If you want to amuse your friends, you will find herein the drollest, queerest quaint and funny jokes imaginable, all suited to the purpose, and almost funny enough to make a wooden image double up with laughter. Send for this book and secure the "real thing" in Dutch comedy. Sent by mail, post-paid, on receipt of **25 Cents.** U. S. postage stamps taken same as cash.

ADDRESS ALL ORDERS TO

HENRY J. WEHMAN, Publisher, 108 Park Row, New York

Popular Books.—Sent post-paid at the Prices Marked

Wehman's Book on Dogs. How to keep and train them. Descriptions of the various breeds, their characteristics and points, and their management in health and disease. Sent by mail, post-paid, on receipt of **10 Cents.**

Wehman's Book on Rabbits. How to breed and manage them. Tells how to arrange their houses, and gives careful instructions as to their food and treatment, both in health and disease. Sent by mail, post-paid, on receipt of **10 Cents.**

Wehman's Book on Pigeons. For pleasure and profit. Tells of the different varieties, both wild and domestic, with full directions for their breeding and care. Sent by mail, post-paid, on receipt of **10 Cents.** U. S. postage stamps taken same as cash.

Wehman's Book on Song Birds. Tells how to rear and treat all the birds that are capable of being domesticated as household songters, in health and disease. Sent by mail, post-paid, on receipt of **10 Cents.** U. S. postage stamps taken same as cash.

Wehman's Book on Pets. Their care and management, including squirrels, guinea pigs, white mice, etc. Also, instructions for aquariums, and the care of silk worms. Sent by mail, post-paid, on receipt of **10 Cents.** U. S. postage stamps taken same as cash.

De Witt's Complete American Farrier and Horse DOCTOR. An American book for American horsemen; with copious notes from the best English and American authorities, showing plainly how to breed, rear, buy, sell, cure, shoe, and keep that most useful and valuable animal, the horse. With many superior illustrations. Sent by mail, post-paid, on receipt of **25 Cents.**

Wehman's Practical Poultry Book. Many old-fashioned farmers are inclined to discredit the statement that there is money in poultry. Why? Because they are not up to the new and improved ideas in poultry management. A little trial of the rules laid down in this book will soon dispel all misgivings in this direction, and tend to convince the most skeptical that there is money in poultry-keeping. Sent by mail, post-paid, on receipt of **25 Cents.**

Wehman's American Live Stock Manual. Many a man has lost a valuable animal for no other reason than he did not know how to take care of it when well, or treat it properly when sick. The cost of this book is but a trifle, but it is simply worth its weight in gold to any man who owns cattle of any kind, for it is a complete text-book, containing the fullest information regarding the rearing of live stock, both in health and disease. Sent by mail, post-paid, on receipt of **25 Cts.**

Wehman's Complete Dancing Master and Call BOOK. All the figures of the German and every new and fashionable dance known in Europe or America. This book is written in so simple a manner that any child, by reading it, can become an expert in dancing without the aid of a teacher. All the latest and fashionable dances are minutely described by illustration from life, explaining positions in round dances, etc., and this original method enables persons to learn the waltz by practicing it a very few times. Hints on the management of balls, etc. Sent by mail, post-paid, on receipt of **25 Cents.**

ADDRESS ALL ORDERS TO

HENRY J. WEHMAN, Publisher, 108 Park Row, New York

Popular Books.—Sent post-paid at the Prices Marked.

Wehman's Book of Crimes and Punishments. As the title suggests, this book tells about crimes and punishments. It is written in an explicit manner, and is a very interesting, as well as instructive, book to read, for it relates facts, not fancies. The following are a few of the subjects treated on in this book:—Russian punishments —Punishing a female with the single knout—Punishment of the double knout—Turkish punishment—Russian soldiers driving exiles into Siberia —Victims of the guillotine—Picketing a girl thirteen years old—Brutal punishment of Englishmen—Depravity of Spanish females—Punishment on the wheel in France—Immolation of a thousand Arabs, and many other subjects equally interesting. Copiously illustrated. Printed on a good quality of paper, from clear, readable type, and bound in handsome colored cover. Price **10 Cents,** by mail, post-paid.

Wehman's Book on Giants and Dwarfs. In most of the ancient histories of the world we read of giants; they also find a place in many of those of modern date, for they are men of extraordinary bulk and stature, and therefore worthy of mention. Dwarfs exist in every country, and there was a time when dwarfs as well as fools shared the favor of courts and the nobility. This book tells of a string of giants and dwarfs and strong men. It also tells of women with beards, horns on human beings, strange effects of anger; also, that deformity is not always a sign of an ill man. It is a very interesting and instructive book, for it relates facts, not fancies. Copiously illustrated with many handsome engravings. Bound in handsome colored cover. Price **10c.,** by mail, post-paid. U. S. postage stamps taken same as cash.

Wehman's Book of Shipwrecks and Adventures on THE OCEAN. Every article in this book is interesting and, therefore, worth reading. It tells of shipwrecks—ships at sea destroyed by running ashore, on rocks, sandbanks, by the force of wind and waves in tempests, and by fire; heroic conduct, perilous situations, and sufferings on the ocean. There is nothing more thrilling to be found in the wildest pages of romance. Parents can safely place this book in the hands of their children, for it relates facts, not fancies. Reading a book of this kind will wean youthful readers *from* pernicious literature, and improve both their understanding and their taste. Copiously illustrated. Bound in handsome colored cover. Price **10 Cents,** by mail, post-paid.

Wehman's Book on Scouts of the West; or, The RIFLE AND THE TOMAHAWK. This book gives an interesting account of American scouts, sent out to gain and bring tidings concerning the movements of Indians. It also tells about Indian scouts, Indians shooting deer, white men fighting with Indians, massacre of white men by Indians, Indian warriors, American scouts drawing the Indians' fire, and a lot of other thrilling adventures of white scouts with the red men in the West. This book relates facts, not fancies, and there is nothing more thrilling to be found in the wildest pages of romance. In short, it is interesting, instructive and cheap. Illustrated with many fine engravings. Printed on a good quality of paper, from clear, readable type, and bound in handsome colored cover. Price **10 Cents,** by mail, post-paid. U. S. postage stamps taken same as cash.

Wehman's Make-Up Book; or, Guide to the Stage. A thorough guide to the art of making up for the stage. Condensed. Practical. Handy. Containing full instructions regarding wigs and beards; make-up material; the various features; age and condition; different nationalities and how to portray them; advice to ladies, etc. By Charles Townsend. Price **25 Cents,** by mail, post-paid.

Popular Books.—Sent post-paid at the Prices Marked.

Wehman's Book of Thrilling Stories about Snakes AND SNAKE CHARMERS. This book tells all about venomous serpents and snake charmers from the earliest days, when the wily serpent in Eden tempted our first mother, Eve, down to the present time. It explains fully why the whole snake tribe have, through all generations and in all countries, inspired the implacable hatred and fear of men, birds, and the brute creation, although the greatest enemy, as well as the greatest victim, has undoubtedly been man. At his hands the snake has no mercy to hope for or expect, and from the snake he, in some unguarded moment, may in an instant receive that wound, whose puncture, though barely larger than the prick of a sharp-pointed needle, is the seal of doom on earth. It would take many times this space to give even a brief idea of its contents. It is interesting and instructive from beginning to end. There is nothing more thrilling to be found in the wildest pages of romance. It relates facts, not fancies. Illustrated with 28 fine engravings. Bound in handsome colored cover. **Price 10c.** per copy, by mail, post-paid.

Wehman's Idle Hours with the Humorists. This book is brimful of fun about Yankee yarns, Western sports, Boarding-house hash—Rich college scrapes—Wild widow's wit, and tall tales of sailors and marines. The following are a few of the titles of pieces contained in this book:—Taking things coolly—The medical student's joke—I'm a corned-beef boarder—Here she goes, there she goes—Sporting with spirits—A surgical operation—How he won the bet?—Encouraging the fine arts—How the Kentuckian came it over the thimble—Back up your cart, madam—The incurable; or, Eat anything—A leap-year story—Popping the question—Can you keep a secret?—A minister and the West Virginia woman, and a whole lot of other exceedingly humorous pieces. There isn't a dull line in the whole book. Worth many times its cost to anyone affected with the blues. and warranted to cure the most obstinate attack. **Price 10 Cents** per copy, by mail, post-paid.

Wehman's Book on Sports and Pastimes of Various NATIONS. The following is a brief synopsis of what this book contains: Explicit treatises on Spanish bull-fights—Hunting the wild bull in Spain—Barbarous sports in Java—Fight between a tiger and a buffalo—The Olympic games of the Greeks—Barbarous sports of the Romans—The dying gladiator—Roman gladiators—Christians exposed to wild beasts, at Rome—Roman chariot race—Equestrian sports of the Mexicans—Blowing up a crocodile—Thrilling sports in the East Indies—Sports of East Indian jugglers—Thrilling sports with bears, etc. This book is well worth any person's time to read, as its contents is so vividly and explicitly described that it cannot fail to interest. It relates facts, not fancies. Copiously illustrated. **Price 10 Cents,** by mail, post-paid.

Wehman's Book on the History of the Horse. Horses are gregarious, and in a wild state inhabit the most retired deserts. In gracefulness of form and dignity of carriage, he appears superior to every other quadruped. This book tells all about the horse from the time of Pharaoh, when Joseph sold grain to the starving people for their money, cattle and horses. Their useful qualities have caused them to be diffused all over the globe. The following is a brief synopsis of its contents, viz.:—Spanish horses—Turkish horses—English horses—Arabian horses—Hungarian horses—Horses in their wild state—Shetland ponies, etc. It also tells how long horses live, and gives records of fleet horses in the past; thrilling feats of horsemanship; stories of the horse; jaguar attacking a horse, etc. This book is copiously illustrated, and is an interesting and instructive book to read. It relates facts, not fancies. **Price 10 Cents** per copy, by mail, post-paid.

ADDRESS ALL ORDERS TO

HENRY J. WEHMAN, Publisher, 108 Park Row, New York.

Popular Books.—Sent post-paid at the Prices Marked

Wehman's Selection of Popular Recitations, No. 1.

This book, the first of the series, contains 88 recitations of wide range of subjects; some full of strength, fire and patriotism; others overflowing with tender feeling and sweet pathos, and still others filled with broad humor and irresistible drollery, and all popular. Recitations appropriate to all occasions will be found in this book. Sent by mail, post-paid, on receipt of **25 Cents.** U. S. postage stamps taken same as cash.

Wehman's Selection of Popular Recitations, No. 2.

This book, the second of the series, contains 89 carefully selected recitations of wide range of subjects; some full of strength, fire and patriotism; others overflowing with tender feeling and sweet pathos, and still others filled with broad humor and irresistible drollery, and all popular. Recitations appropriate to all occasions will be found in this book. This selection of pieces is entirely different from No. 1. Sent by mail, post-paid, on receipt of **25 Cents.** U. S. postage stamps taken same as cash.

Wehman's Selection of Popular Recitations, No. 3.

This book, the third of the series, contains 88 carefully selected recitations of wide range of subjects; some full of strength, fire and patriotism; others overflowing with tender feeling and sweet pathos, and still others filled with broad humor and irresistible drollery, and all popular. Recitations appropriate to all occasions will be found in this book. This selection of pieces is entirely different from Nos. 1 and 2. Sent by mail, post-paid, on receipt of **25 Cents.** Clean and unused United States postage stamps taken same as cash.

Wehman's Selection of Popular Recitations, No. 4.

This book, the fourth of the series, contains 94 carefully selected recitations of wide range of subjects; some full of strength, fire and patriotism; others overflowing with tender feeling and sweet pathos, and still others filled with broad humor and irresistible drollery, and all popular. Recitations appropriate to all occasions will be found in this book. This selection of pieces is entirely different from Nos. 1, 2 and 3. Sent by mail, post-paid, on receipt of **25 Cents.** Clean and unused United States postage stamps taken same as cash.

Gus Williams' Fireside Recitations, No. 1.

This book, the first of the series, contains 95 of the purest and most interesting and effective pieces in prose and poetry in the language. Many of the articles in this book have been recited by the compiler, with every mark of approval, before large audiences. While many of the favorite standard pieces are retained, the majority are those newer and fresher productions that are difficult, if not impossible, to find in any one volume. Sent by mail, post-paid, on receipt of **25 Cents.**

Gus Williams' Fireside Recitations, No. 2.

This book, the second of the series, contains a choice collection of 96 pieces in prose and poetry, especially adapted for reading and speaking by the members of refined, select home circles. It must be remembered that because Mr. Williams is a very FUNNY man, it by no means follows that he is merely a funny man. Humor is but one side of his diversified character; he is as noted for his fine perception and delineation of more serious sentiments. He knows exactly the kind of article to start a hearty laugh, or —as in this work—to beguile us of our tears. Sent by mail, post-paid, on receipt of **25 Cents.** U. S. postage stamps taken same as cash.

ADDRESS ALL ORDERS TO

HENRY J. WEHMAN, Publisher, 108 Park Row, New York

Popular Books.—Sent post-paid at the Prices Marked.

Webster's Little Folks' Speaker. Comprising many standard pieces, as well as a great many original compositions, embracing a wide range of subjects. This book is well printed, from clear, readable type, and bound in durable, handsome, colored paper cover. Sent by mail, post-paid, on receipt of **25 Cents.**

De Witt's Superior School Speaker. A successful effort has been made to render this superior to any published. There are many fresh, hearty, original pieces in the work, that will impress and delight all lovers of spirited speaking. Sent by mail, post-paid, on receipt of **10 Cents.** U. S. postage stamps taken same as cash.

De Witt's Public School Speaker. Containing a selection of the choicest pieces for recitation in public schools, academies, etc. This book is in the ascending scale—the sentiments, style, and lessons taught are all of a higher grade than those of the "Primary School Speaker." Sent by mail, post-paid, on receipt of **10 Cents.**

De Witt's Choice School Speaker. The pieces in this book are most carefully chosen from many hundreds of the best pieces. Any one having a copy of this book will never be at loss for fine specimens of interesting and animated speaking. Sent by mail, post-paid, on receipt of **10 Cents.** U. S. postage stamps taken same as cash.

Wehman's Little Folks' Stories. A charming book, which will afford the little folks many an evening's entertainment and amusement. It contains twenty entirely original stories, embracing a wide range of subjects, beautifully illustrated by the justly celebrated artist, Paul Konewka. Sent by mail, post-paid, on receipt of **25 Cents.**

De Witt's Advanced School Speaker. Adapted particularly to those pupils who give proof that they have the ability to become good readers. There is a fine assortment of excellent pieces in this Speaker, many of them American in every sense. Sent by mail, post-paid, on receipt of **10 Cents.** U. S. postage stamps taken same as cash.

Prescott's Paragon Reciter. An unusually fine collection of fresh and original pieces, as well as standard selections of prose and poetry, suitable for recitation and declamation in the higher classes of schools and seminaries. This book is well printed on good, substantial paper, from clear, readable type, and bound in handsome, durable colored paper. Sent by mail, post-paid, on receipt of **25 Cents.**

Prescott's Standard Recitations. Gathered with great care from the best American and English specimens of first-class pieces for speaking in schools, and for the home recreation and improvement. This book is well printed on fine quality book paper, from clear, readable type, and bound in handsome colored paper. Sent by mail, post-paid, on receipt of **25 Cents.** U. S. postage stamps taken same as cash.

Prescott's Social Readings and Recitations. A collection of excellent pieces of wide range of subjects; some full of strength, fire and patriotism; others overflowing with tender feeling and sweet pathos, and still others filled with broad humor and irresistible drollery. For use in schools and lyceums, or by the home fireside. Well printed on good, substantial book paper, from clear, readable type, and bound in attractive, heavy, colored cover. Sent by mail, post-paid, on receipt of **25 Cents.** U. S. postage stamps taken same as cash.

ADDRESS ALL ORDERS TO

HENRY J. WEHMAN, Publisher, 108 Park Row, New York.

Popular Books.—Sent post-paid at the Prices Marked

De Witt's Handy Letter Writer. Containing full and explicit instructions in the art of letter writing, with many hints as to style, composition, and punctuation of letters on a variety of subjects, from business to pleasure. Sent by mail, post-paid, on receipt of **10 cts.**

Webster's Practical Letter Writer. Containing general directions for writing. Also, model letters, family letters, children's letters, letters of friendship, letters of sympathy, love letters, letters of distinguished men and women, business letters, letters of introduction, and model notes of invitation. Together with Bible quotations, choice prose and poetical quotations, Latin, French, Spanish and Italian words and phrases, synonyms, abbreviations, mottoes of the States, and model of printer's proof corrections. Sent by mail, post-paid, on receipt of **25 Cents.**

Webster's Ready-Made Love Letters. Comprising notes and letters of every style tor almost every conceivable occasion, from first acquaintance to marriage, with invaluable information on the etiquette of courtship. Also, model letters from some of the world's most famous lovers, and a large number of appropriate poetical quotations from standard authors. The whole forming a convenient aid to those who need friendly counsel and confidential advice in matters pertaining to love and courtship. Sent by mail, post-paid, on receipt of **25 Cents.** U. S. postage stamps taken same as cash.

Wehman's Business Letter Writer. This book contains a large variety of carefully selected specimen business letters; also a large number of legal and mercantile forms used in business, such as Articles of Co-partnership—Notice of Dissolution—Form of an Assignment, Acknowledgment of Deed, Bill of Sale, Power of Attorney—Judgment Note, etc. In commercial circles letter writing is an important matter, as great interests are involved in business letters, and results of gain or loss are dependent upon them. Sent by mail, post-paid, on receipt of **25 Cents.** United States postage stamps taken as cash.

Wehman's Complete Letter Writer. Shows clearly all the blunders and mistakes apt to be made by an inexperienced writer, and makes manifest in the simplest way the proper method of avoiding them, whether they occur in the spelling, the punctuation, or the grammar. There are in this book valuable hints on Love, Courtship and Marriage, showing in detail in what style lovers should indite epistles. Also, an IMPORTANT FEATURE, namely, the legal importance of a letter; and explanations are given upon the exact meaning of expressions used in writing that may be brought into court in litigation. Sent by mail, post-paid, on receipt of **25 Cents.**

Wehman's Book of Love Letters. Love and courtship letters should be an index of the writer's good sense and judgment, as well as the state of the affections, and therefore regard should be had, in the composition of them. And though in persons of refinement and education an honorable attachment will suffice to prompt its candid expression, there are many persons not possessed of these advantages, to whom correspondence is always attended with considerable difficulty. To all such the series of letters contained in this book, in which delicacy of feeling, and the warmth of expression suited to the subject have been carefully blended, will be found an important aid in acquiring facility and accuracy in the art of letter-writing. It also contains the art of Secret Writing, the language of love poetically portrayed, and simplified rules of grammar. Sent by mail, post-paid, on receipt of **25 Cents.**

ADDRESS ALL ORDERS TO

HENRY J. WEHMAN, Publisher, 108 Park Row, New York

Popular Books.—Sent post-paid at the Prices Marked

Wehman's Italian without a Teacher. A new system, on the most simple principles for universal self-tuition, with complete English pronunciation of every word. By Franz Thimm. With the aid of this book any person can acquire a thorough knowledge of the Italian language in a very short time, as the method of learning is so simple that a child could understand it. If you are desirous of learning to speak the Italian language, you cannot make a better investment. This book is printed on a good quality of paper, from clear, readable type, and is bound in a handsome colored cover. Compared with its intrinsic value, the price of this book is but a nominal one. Price 25c. per copy, by mail, post-paid.

Wehman's German without a Teacher. A new system, on the most simple principles, for universal self-tuition, with complete English pronunciation of every word. Next to our own, the German language is the most prevalent in this country to-day, as a large percentage of our population are either Germans or of German extraction, therefore the German language is worth knowing. With the aid of this book any person can acquire a thorough knowledge of the German language, as the method for learning is so simple that a child could understand it. This edition has been revised and corrected by H. A. C. Anderson, M.D. It is simply worth its weight in gold. Price 25 Cents per copy, by mail, post-paid.

Wehman's French without a Teacher. A new system, on the most simple principles, for universal self-tuition, with complete English pronunciation of every word, table of coins, etc. With the aid of this book any person can acquire a thorough knowledge of the French language in a very short time. This book has been revised by Prof. M. Gauthier, and no pains or expense, consistent with its price, has been spared to make it a book that every person desirous of learning French will be happy to possess. Printed on a good quality of paper, from clear, readable type, and bound in handsome colored cover. Price 25 Cents per copy, by mail, post-paid.

Wehman's Spanish without a Teacher. A new system on the most simple principles for universal self-tuition, with complete English pronunciation of every word. By Franz Thimm. With the aid of this book any person can acquire a thorough knowledge of the Spanish language in a very short time, as the method of learning is so simple that a child could understand it. Now, more than ever before, the Spanish language is worth knowing, for the reason that America, through conquest in war, has come into possession of territory formerly under the sovereignty of Spain, and where for centuries the Spanish language has been spoken, and which will henceforth be governed by America. Therefore Americans will find it advantageous to know the Spanish language before embarking to these "new fertile fields" for American ingenuity, as it will be many years before the native population of this newly-acquired territory will understand our language. Price 25 Cents per copy, by mail, post-paid.

Wehman's Book on the History of the Heroes. "Hero worship exists, has existed, and will forever exist universally among mankind." This book tells of men of distinguished valor and enterprise in danger and fortitude in suffering; also of Indian Warriors—Indian Depredations—Female Captives Going Into Captivity—Women Captives Pleading for Mercy—Massacre of Women, and many other thrilling adventures with the Red man. This book relates facts, not fancies, and there is nothing more thrilling to be found in the wildest pages of romance. It is interesting and instructive, and illustrated with many handsome engravings. Price 10 Cents, by mail, post-paid.

ADDRESS ALL ORDERS TO
HENRY J. WEHMAN, Publisher, 108 Park Row, New York.

www.ingramcontent.com/pod-product-compliance
Lightning Source LLC
LaVergne TN
LVHW041156080426
835511LV00006B/629